COPERNICUS

Born: February 19, 1473

Died: May 24, 1543

Regarded as the founder of modern astronomy, Copernicus was one of the most versatile geniuses of the sixteenth century—astronomer, physician, churchman, soldier and philosopher. He defied the thinkers of his day and inspired one of the great revolutions in human thought. Overthrowing the age-old belief that the earth was fixed at the center of the universe, he established the theory that the earth rotates daily on its axis and the planets revolve in orbits around the sun.

Copernicus

by Henry Thomas

Julian Messner   New York

Published simultaneously in the United States and Canada by
Julian Messner, a division of Simon & Schuster, Inc.,
1 West 39 Street, New York, N.Y. All rights reserved.

Fifth Printing, 1967

Printed in the United States of America
Library of Congress Catalog Card No. 60–13265

Chapter 1

IN 1939, WHEN THE NAZIS overran Poland, they looted and murdered the inhabitants without mercy. The scene of one of their most savage atrocities was the University of Kraków, the alma mater of Copernicus. The head of the German occupational army had made an announcement that one of their scientists would hold a lecture at that university. The proposed subject of the lecture was "The Attitude of the Nazis toward Higher Learning."

When the audience had assembled for the lecture, the Nazi soldiers surrounded the building and the speaker stepped upon the platform with the following proclamation:

"Since most of you understand German, it will not be necessary for me to have my message translated into Polish. Because you have kept the university open without our knowledge or consent, because you have continued your laboratory experiments and conducted your examinations without our approval, and finally, because this university has always been a bastion of what you call Polish culture, you are all under arrest."

The speaker ordered the door flung open and Nazi soldiers stormed into the lecture hall. Among those arrested were about two hundred professors. The prisoners were thrown into lorries and carried off to an unknown destination. Within a few weeks the ashes of several of the professors began to arrive in urns. Many of the others died later in concentration camps or came back to die at home as a result of their brutal treatment.

The Polish professors attending the lecture had been seized under the portrait of Copernicus that graced one of the walls in the assembly room. This portrait was a symbolic reminder of a strange historic parallel to the Nazi atrocity. It happened about four hundred years earlier, with Copernicus himself a prime figure during a similar attempt to overrun Poland. In the sixteenth century the Teutonic Knights, a military religious order, entered upon a crusade to establish their "Nordic supremacy" in Poland. In the course of their plunder they came upon the Castle of Allenstein—a stronghold of the Polish church in which Copernicus served as a canon and teacher.

At the approach of the Teutonic Knights many of the religious members of the castle had fled. Copernicus was among the few who refused to run away; nor did he stand idly by while the marauders were devastating the countryside. Instead he sent a message to King Sigismund I of Poland asking him for military help. Age forty-seven at the time, Copernicus had never been trained as a soldier. He was interested in the motions of the stars rather than in the commotions of men. But when his country was in danger, he was ready to help defend her.

With the help of the king he fortified the castle, raised a company of citizen soldiers and faced the Teutonic Knights. Their Grand Master declared that he was determined "to destroy the nest of Polish perversion so that no bird could nestle there." He burned down the surrounding villages, slaughtered the men and drove the women and children into exile.

Their main target, however, was "the crazy astronomer who dared to defy the sun in the heavens and the Master

9

of the Teutonic Knights on earth." They laid siege to the castle and prepared lampoons against the "subversive" ideas of Copernicus. They depicted him as a clownish cook who rotated a fowl (the earth) on a spit around a blazing fire (the sun). They burned him in effigy and looked forward to the day when they could burn him in person.

But Copernicus continued to resist the enemy, and repelled their repeated assaults for several months. Burdened as he was with the pressing responsibilities of Church and country, he nevertheless found time to conduct his scientific work, as recorded astronomical observations—dated from February to July, 1520, the height of the siege—prove.

Finally the Master of the Teutonic Knights was compelled to withdraw his troops. Only then did Copernicus lay down his armor and return to his peaceful canonical duties. Thus he was saved for the writing of the book that marked the birth of modern science.

As he sat working on his book, *Concerning the Revolutions of the Heavenly Spheres,* Copernicus paused at times to think of the events that had helped to shape his life. What was it that had turned his mind to so many different interests? He recalled some of his childhood experiences—his first awareness of the turbulence of men and the quietude of the stars.

Nicolas Koppernig—he used the Latin form, Copernicus, in later years—spent his boyhood in Torún, a city fortified against external invasions and attacked by internal plagues. His father was a well-to-do copper merchant. Nicolas, born on February 19, 1473, was the youngest of four children—two girls and two boys. The family lived in a house within the heavy walls of the city on the right bank of the Vistula.

This river was a highway of busy traffic between Poland and Hungary on the one hand and western Europe on the other. Koppernig frequently took his children down to the wharves to watch the ships arriving and departing with their cargoes of metal, pottery, pitch, wax, salt herring, cloth, silk and spices. The whole world seemed to be passing before the wondering eyes of the children.

On week ends and holidays the Koppernigs drove out to a vineyard they owned on the outskirts of Torún. This district, unprotected by towers or ramparts, was occupied by peasants who tilled the fields and by laborers who could not afford to live within the walls of the city.

Nicolas enjoyed his visits to the countryside. But when he went into the hut of Stan Kozlovsky, the gardener

11

who took care of his father's vineyard, he had to hold his nose. The entire Kozlovsky family—father, mother and three children—lived in one room. And in addition to the family, there were several other occupants: a pig, a goat and a number of hens. The air inside was so stifling it made Nicolas sick. Their own house in the city was so big and spacious and clean. Nicolas often wondered about the difference between the houses of the rich and the hovels of the poor.

"Why can't the Kozlovskys," he asked his father, "have a big house like ours to live in?"

"Because they are poor," replied his father. "They can't afford to build houses with room enough for everybody."

It was generally in the evening that the Koppernigs started back from their vineyard to the city. As they stepped out of the gardener's hut, the little boy would draw a deep breath and look up into the sky. So much room for the stars up there, so little room for the poor down here. It was a pleasant trip over the dark roads of the countryside. But wouldn't it be even more pleasant, thought Nicolas, to travel over the dark sky from star to star?

The stars were a frequent subject of conversation in the Koppernig family. Almost everybody in those days believed in astrology. If a person was sick, or failed in business, or lost his house in a fire, or died in an accident, he was said to have been born under an unlucky star. Koppernig was a successful merchant, he told his family, because the stars had smiled down upon the world at the time of his birth.

Nicolas' mother was also a firm believer in astrology. One of the most beautiful women in Poland, she ascribed her beauty to the "harmonious conjunction of the constellations" when she was a little girl. As a child, Nicolas did not understand the meaning of such words as "harmonious," "conjunction" and "constellation," but they seemed to have a deep meaning. At any rate, the conversations on astrology he heard at home directed his attention to the mystery of the heavens.

Nicolas received a different opinion about the heavens from his mother's brother, Lucas Watzelrode. Uncle Lucas had been a schoolteacher for a number of years, then became a Catholic priest. On his frequent visits to the Koppernigs, he laughed at their addiction to astrology, which he dismissed as a sham science.

"The real science of the heavens," he told them, "is astronomy; and the motions of the stars as described in the books on astronomy have nothing to do with the affairs of men. God alone is the arbiter of our fate."

These words made a profound impression upon the sensitive mind of Nicolas. Other impressions became

13

fixed through a series of dramatic events—the attack upon the Koppernig vineyard by a band of robbers, the murder of Kozlovsky and the massacre of a number of Jews who lived in the ghetto in Torún. There was altogether too much brutality and suffering in the world, thought young Nicolas.

An epidemic of smallpox broke out in the city, and within a few weeks a great many of the inhabitants died. Uncle Lucas was kept busy ministering to the spiritual needs of the sick. He told the Koppernigs that one of the saddest things about the plague was the scarcity of doctors.

"There are plenty of quacks," he said, "who pretend to cure people with magic incantations and the powdered bones of cats and dogs. What we need, however, is more men trained in the science of medicine."

That became another subject of deep interest for Nicolas, especially after his brother, Andreas, was stricken in the plague. Fortunately he survived; but he was left so weak and puny that, though older than Nicolas, he looked like his younger brother.

There were so many cruelties that had to be stopped, so many sufferers who needed to be helped, so many mysteries that begged to be solved. If a man could only be and do all things at once! "That's the sort of man I'd like to become," Nicolas confided to his uncle.

14

Lucas Watzelrode stroked his nephew's tousled head. "Just try to become a good man, Nicolas," he said. "On a foundation of goodness you can build all kinds of splendid careers."

When Nicolas was ten, his father died and Lucas asked his sister and her children to come and live with him. He took them into his home and heart and directed the education of the children. It was under the influence of Lucas Watzelrode that Nicolas was able to develop the three predominant traits of his character—piety, pity and wonder at the mystery of the world.

Chapter 2

LUCAS WATZELRODE first sent Nicolas to St. John's, a grammar school where he himself had taught for a number of years. Later he enrolled his nephew at the Cathedral Academy on the Vistula, some miles away from Torún. This was a preparatory school for the priesthood.

The head of the academy was a teacher with a great sense of humor. His name was Vodka, which means brandy; but he Latinized it in accordance with the com-

mon practice among the scholars of the period. The name he assumed, however, was not *Vodkius* (brandy drinker) but *Abstemius* (abstainer).

Dr. Abstemius was a slight, pale and nervous little teacher who bustled about the classroom in the shabbiest of clothes. When called to task about his careless dress, he replied, "My clothes are like my person. A plain message doesn't require an elegant envelope."

The teachers and the students of the academy got up every morning at dawn, when the bugle sounded the Heynal, or Sunrise Hymn. This hymn was the famous "Broken Melody" of Poland. It commemorated the heroism of the Trumpeter of Kraków. Everyone in Poland knew the legend, but Dr. Abstemius always retold it to his new pupils:

"Many years before your day, during the Tatar invasion of Poland in 1241, it was the custom for the official Trumpeter of Kraków to keep watch on the tower of the Church of Our Lady Mary, and to sound the warning when he saw the enemy's approach toward the city.

"The church was situated upon a high hill on the outskirts of the city. It was a lonely and perilous spot for the Trumpeter. Every day the fugitives from the surrounding towns and villages, flocking past the church toward the shelter of Kraków, reported that the Tatars were drawing closer and sweeping everything before

17

them. They were a savage horde, these Tatars, dressed in the skins of animals, galloping upon their swift, small horses, bent upon murder and plunder and rape.

"At last the approach of the enemy could be seen from the church tower. A cloud of smoke came rolling in from the horizon, and here and there the roof of a burning farmhouse shot a sudden tongue of flame toward the sky.

"For a moment the Trumpeter was panic-stricken. He was little more than a boy, only nineteen or so. Perhaps it would be best to join the refugees and escape into the city!

"But no. He had sworn to remain at his post until the end. From his high platform on the hilltop he could see the enemy some time before they became visible to the defenders of Kraków. He must give the warning without delay, so his people would be ready for the attack.

"Raising the trumpet to his lips, he began to play the Heynal. The Sunrise Song of Poland! Whatever attacks his country might face, her sun would rise again and again!

"The Tatars had now reached the foot of the hill. One of their bowmen dropped to his knee, took careful aim and shot an arrow toward the tower on the summit. It flew straight to the mark and pierced the Trumpeter's breast. He was unable to finish the song. One last tri-

umphant note in the middle of a phrase and the gallant
young soldier fell dead.

"His body went up in flames as the Tatars set fire to
the wooden church. But his countrymen had been
alerted; and his 'Broken Melody' is ringing down the
ages to remind us of our heroic past."

The story of the "Broken Melody" never failed to
arouse the patriotic fervor of Nicolas Koppernig. Yet, in
addition to his sense of patriotism, he grew up with a
feeling of world unity as a result of his training at the
Cathedral Academy. Dr. Abstemius impressed upon his
pupils the importance of the religious brotherhood of the
Church and the universal fellowship of learning.

"In the sovereignty of the Church," Dr. Abstemius reminded his pupils, "all men are equal under one God.
And in the dominion of Learning, all scholars are indebted to one language." Latin was the universal language used in most European countries for the training
of scholars and the writing of books. In this way the boys
in the Cathedral Academy imbibed a strong superna-
tional feeling in which their ardor was like a sunbeam
that streamed out of an all-embracing light.

Dr. Abstemius frequently brought this idea home to
his pupils. "Many countries but one world," was among
his favorite expressions, "many worlds but one universe."
He frequently called to their attention the words of

19

Dante. "My homeland," said this great religious poet, "is the world itself. Can I not see the sun and the stars shine everywhere? Can I not everywhere ponder upon the noblest truths?"

Thus, under the guidance of Dr. Abstemius, Nicolas learned to regard himself as a lover of his homeland but a citizen of the universe. His teacher, like himself, was interested in astronomy. Together they took evening strolls along the banks of the Vistula and talked about the silent mystery of the stars.

"If only I could penetrate their silence and reveal their story to the world!" Nicolas said one night.

His teacher replied, "Perhaps you will, Nicolas. You have the vision and the gift of words."

The headmaster's interest in astronomy had begun in his more mature years. As a young man he had shared the popular belief in astrology. But as a student at the University of Kraków under the famous astronomer Professor Brudzewski, he had become disillusioned about the unscientific theories of the astrologers. Again and again, referring to the supposed influence of the heavenly bodies upon human events, Professor Brudzewski had declared, "Don't blame the stars but your own frailties for your sicknesses and your sins."

Dr. Abstemius spoke often about his famous professor. "When you get into the University of Kraków," he told

Nicolas, "be sure to take several courses under this man."

In the meantime Nicolas and his teacher made a number of astronomical observations at the Cathedral Academy. They constructed a gnomon, or crude sundial, and a Jacob's staff—a stick with two movable crossbars for measuring the movements of the planets from the angles which the planets made with the earth—and with the help of these simple instruments they charted their course in what they called their "little excursions into the sky." Some of the superstitious people in the neighborhood shook their heads at the sight of these strange instruments. They began to spread a rumor that the teacher was a sort of magician. They said that he had created an iron fly which he could send zooming through the air and bring back to his hand by beckoning to it with his finger.

Dr. Abstemius laughed when he heard the story. "There's not the slightest truth in it," he said. "I couldn't make a lifeless toy obey me with the mere motion of a finger. I can't even make my living pupils obey me without the contact of my hand upon their backside."

There was nothing of the charlatan about the wise and witty headmaster of the Cathedral Academy. This man, with his subtle sense of humor and his intellectual interests, shaped the mind of Nicolas into lofty thoughts just as a master sculptor shapes his clay into noble lines.

Under Dr. Abstemius' tuition the young student learned to turn his gaze toward eternal things.

Under the guidance of his uncle, the boy developed a practical outlook upon the material as well as the spiritual needs of life. Lucas Watzelrode was not only a scholar but a man of the world. He was consecrated Bishop of Ermland when Nicolas was sixteen, and moved into a palace close to the Gulf of Danzig. He appointed a number of canons, or church officers, to collect the rents from the peasants and to administer the government of the diocese. "When you have completed your education," he said to Nicolas, "I shall appoint you one of my canons. That office will give you a better livelihood and a wider scope for your talents than a mere priesthood."

Thus Nicolas had a definite job awaiting him when he entered the University of Kraków. At the time of his enrollment, in 1491, he was eighteen years old.

He was not quite certain as to the course he was to pursue. His interests were wide and varied—he wanted to serve God, study the stars and help mankind. Theology, astronomy, medicine, how was he to choose among the three? Fortunately one of his new teachers, Conrad Celtes, was able to guide him in the right direction.

Dr. Celtes was a disciple of the astronomer Brudzewski, who had retired from teaching just before Nicolas' arrival at the university. But, in addition to his esteem for Brudzewski, Dr. Celtes had learned to admire the Humanists, the European scholars whose studies embraced the entire field of human endeavor. "Why don't you apply yourself to a variety of subjects at the university?" he suggested to Nicolas. "There's no reason why you can't be a good theologian, astronomer and doctor at the same time."

Nicolas accepted his teacher's advice and enrolled himself as a "student of humane learning." He and Celtes became good friends. The two young men—Celtes was only about ten years older than Nicolas—roamed the streets of Kraków, visited an occasional tavern, slid down a rope to explore the neighboring salt mines, got into scrapes between the citizens and the students—"the townsmen and the gownsmen"—and wrote Latin verses to the pretty girls of the city.

Now and then they ran into a group of sailors who told them about perilous voyages in which they had only the stars to guide them. Professor Brudzewski, as Celtes confided to Nicolas, held a strange theory about the stars. In his private conversations with his intimate friends he expressed his belief that the sun did not move around the earth—as the early astronomers had declared—but that the earth moved around the sun. Yet Brudzewski never uttered this dangerous new doctrine in public. It might cost him his job—or even his life.

Little by little Nicolas was beginning to understand why it was dangerous to give voice to new theories—aside from the fact that people usually fear things they cannot comprehend. During the Middle Ages the spirit of learning was kept alive in monasteries and churches, around which schools slowly grew. Among the treasures that Western scholars valued most highly were copies of Ptolemy's *Almagest* (a comprehensive outline of Greek astronomy) and many of Aristotle's scientific as well as philosophical writings. Since the validity of Aristotelian logic was not questioned, the scientific subjects were accepted as equally true. In time the Greeks' geocentric notion of the universe was incorporated into the official philosophy of the Church, and anyone who questioned the theory that the sun revolved around the earth found himself in direct opposition to Christian theology and the religious authorities.

Nicolas gave much thought to Brudzewski's idea as explained by Celtes. "As you know," said Celtes, "the astronomical system of Ptolemy is based upon a complicated motion of celestial circles within circles, circles crisscrossing one another and circles whirling erratically away from other circles."

"Yes," Nicolas replied quickly. "You are referring to his cycles, epicycles, deferents and excentrics."

Celtes nodded. "These terms are supposed to explain everything in the universe. Yet they actually explain nothing. Whenever Ptolemy couldn't account for the motion of a planet in an *actual* circle, he put it into an *imaginary* circle. And thus his astronomy is a fictitious rather than a real picture of the world."

"For myself," said Nicolas, "I prefer to find one simple formula that will explain all the movements of the planets and the stars."

"This is precisely the idea of Professor Brudzewski!" exclaimed Celtes. "And he believes he has discovered this formula in the motion of the earth around the sun!"

That conversation made a profound impression upon Nicolas. The Ptolemaic system, over a thousand years old, was still accepted as the truth, even though, according to that system, the planets failed to move in a definite design. They frequently appeared in positions where they had no business to be. Nicolas decided that there was something radically wrong with the discrepancies in the planetary movements and he told himself that he would have to look into this matter—sometime in the future. For the present there were too many other interests that occupied his thoughts. He especially enjoyed the debates among the students. In those days the chief collegiate sports were mental gymnastics rather than physical games. Every Saturday there was a debate open to the public and attended by crowds of enthusiastic partisans. Some of the subjects for the debates were rather naïve:

"Can God undo something He has done—for instance, turn a criminal into a saint?"

"Why did Adam eat an apple instead of a pear?"

"How many angels can sit on the head of a needle?"

"Can you save a heretic's soul by burning his body?"

Other topics, especially those selected by the more serious students, provided mental exercise of a better sort:

"Which is the truer philosophy—Plato's or Aristotle's?"

"Was Maimonides right when he declared that the best kind of charity is to abolish poverty so that there will be no need for charity?"

"What has produced the greater good—Alexander's sword or Homer's pen?"

At times the debates became so heated that the students left the lecture room and fought out the issue in a duel.

It was a restless period during which Nicolas attended the university. Kraków, "the international capital of East and West," was a city of palaces and hovels, courtiers and beggars, merchants and artisans and peasants and peddlers, alchemists who tried to transmute baser metals into gold and tutors who tried to transform inferior brains into educated minds. As Nicolas strolled through the streets on market days, he had a chance to observe people from many parts of the world—Tatars, Turks, Cossacks, Czechs, Italians, Slovaks, Ruthenians, Moors, Flemings and Germans. He often exchanged ideas with those whose language he could speak. And time and again he conversed with foreign professors who visited the university. From all these contacts he derived as much knowledge about the problems of his day as he absorbed from his books about the wisdom of the past.

In the late fifteenth century the life of a student was not an isolated sojourn in an ivory tower. It was an active participation in the affairs of the outside world. This, at least, was certainly the case with Nicolas Koppernig. One of his sisters had married a merchant of Kraków. His brother-in-law frequently consulted him about serious business problems, for he recognized the unusual keenness of Koppernig's mind. Through these discussions Nicolas became interested in economics—the principles of buying and selling, of coinage, inflation and deflation, and of the general conditions that determined periods of plenty and times of want. In later years he had occasion to apply the knowledge he had gained while helping his brother-in-law.

In his second year at Kraków there arose a crisis that demanded his immediate attention. A fire broke out in the university section of the city. The alarm sounded in the middle of the night as the flames swept down the street in the direction of the main building of the university. The burning houses, mostly of wood and huddled closely together, turned into a raging furnace of destruction that threatened the entire city. Nicolas, at the head of a company of volunteer students, joined the fire wardens of Kraków. They commandeered a number of wagons, piled them with empty tubs and buckets and drove them to a nearby reservoir, where they filled them with water and hurried back to the roaring inferno. Since there were not enough horses to go around, a number of the citizens and students harnessed themselves into the shafts and pulled the wagons to and from the reservoir.

The flames, fanned by a stiff breeze, gained steady headway. "Tear down the houses nearest the fire!" shouted the captain of the wardens. In a short time the wholesale demolition of the houses with hooks and axes and battering-rams added further confusion to the havoc wrought by the fire.

The flames had now reached some of the dormitories of the students. Books and manuscripts were rushed into the streets and carried to places of safety, but at times the fire outraced the rescuers and many precious documents were destroyed in a hurricane of blazing sparks.

Through all this turmoil Nicolas Koppernig remained calm, directing his company of students with a firm hand. His main purpose was to bring order out of chaos. Again and again he stopped to quiet a milling crowd, to put a soothing hand on the shoulder of a hysterical woman, to lead a frightened child away from the danger zone.

At last the fire was controlled—not, however, before it had destroyed two of the university buildings. Here and there a ruin kept smoldering for many hours, but the heart of the fire had been confined to a district surrounded by a wide ring of demolished buildings and flooded with a deluge of water that had been brought up from the reservoir.

The day after the conflagration Conrad Celtes met Nicolas with a long face. "I lost one of my most precious possessions in the fire—a comedy of Plautus which I had dug up in the ruins of Pompeii. I was planning to have it published. So far as I know, my manuscript was the only copy of this comedy in existence."

"And I," said Koppernig, "lost all my notes on the philosophy of Aristotle."

Celtes shook his head in bewilderment. His training under some of the leading scholars of the day had given

29

him a skeptical outlook on life. "Man toils," he said, "and God spoils."

"Can you explain it?" asked Nicolas. "Why is there all this evil and destruction and pain in a beautiful world?"

"That's for you to explain," retorted Celtes. "You're the theologian, you know."

"As I see it," said Koppernig, trying to answer his own question, "the world has been designed by a supreme Artist. What you and I see is but a thread here and there —birth, death, joy, sorrow, success, failure, a heap of dust and a handful of stars. But even from the little we see we realize that all these threads are woven into a perfect design. I believe that every life, every leaf on every tree and each single grain of sand, is patterned by a Mind of infinite wisdom and infinite love. So let us have faith that He who has designed the whole has not overlooked any of the parts. I believe that every life has had a beginning long before birth and will continue long after death. This is what I mean when I talk about the pattern of the world."

"I wonder," said Celtes.

"So do I, to tell the truth. But let us not, for heaven's sake, ever give up this sense of wonder. It is the spur that keeps us forever on the quest for a better understanding of the world we live in."

Thus Koppernig continued his studies at Kraków,

yielding now and then to a moment of doubt but gaining many experiences that built his character and expanded his mind.

Then came astounding information that set Koppernig's imagination on fire. An Italian explorer, pushing out into the unknown and braving the terrors of uncharted seas for many days, had finally discovered what appeared to be a new world! The name of the intrepid navigator was Cristoforo Colombo. This amazing discovery suggested to Nicolas that there were many new worlds to explore—not only on the sea but in the heavens as well.

Chapter 3

ALTHOUGH A BRILLIANT STUDENT, Nicolas was not very popular with some of his teachers. He asked too many questions that they were unable to answer, and he had a habit of expressing ideas that threatened to upset their conventional way of life. It became almost too dangerous for a teacher to be caught conversing with this young rebel.

The only one who dared to remain his intimate friend

was Celtes. Yet even this teacher, though liberal in his thoughts, warned Nicolas to hold his tongue when he spoke to the ruling authorities of the university.

"There are two things you must accept," cautioned Celtes, "if you want to live undisturbed. They are the tradition of the Church and the astronomy of Ptolemy."

"As far as the Church is concerned," Nicolas replied, "I accept its teaching with all my heart. But when it comes to Ptolemy, I want to use my own judgment. I prefer to figure out for myself how much of his theory I can accept. This, I believe, is why God has given me a mind— to think before I decide."

"So you want to be a martyr?"

"I didn't say that. But I do want to seek the truth. I've been reading quite a number of books on astronomy, which have raised some serious doubts in my mind. Some of the ancient scientists, you'll recall, held different views from those of Ptolemy. Pythagoras said that the earth is a sphere floating in space. And Philolaus believed that the center of the universe is a huge fire around which the earth revolves."

Celtes nodded. "But," he pointed out, "their theories have been rejected for almost two thousand years, and Ptolemy has been accepted in their place."

"Haven't you told me that your own friend Professor

Brudzewski, suspected that the sun, rather than the earth, is the center of the universe?"

"Privately, yes—but as a rule he kept this suspicion to himself. And if you are wise, Nicolas, you will do the same."

"It is the part of wisdom," protested Nicolas, "to seek the truth."

Celtes looked at him with a quizzical smile. There was pity as well as admiration in his eyes. "The seekers of truth," he said gently, "have a hard road to travel." He was worried about his young friend, but he said nothing more on the subject at the time.

Nicolas did not take his teacher's advice. He continued to express his ideas, not only on astronomy but on every subject under the sun. As a result he became a rather lonely figure. The more timid among the students followed the lead of their professors and avoided him.

"Don't get too close to him," quipped one of the students to his companions, "or he'll whisk you away on a spin around the stars."

"Or drag you along with him into the torture chambers of the Inquisition," another student added.

The dreaded Roman Inquisition was an ever-present threat during the Middle Ages. The officers of this investigating tribunal of the Church were empowered to seek out and punish all those who held views contrary to orthodox belief. Thousands of people whose only crime was to think for themselves were burned at the stake through the persecution of the Inquisitors. At one time Nicolas' own father, in an effort to escape arrest as a suspected heretic, had offered to spy for the Inquisition. Even though it was for his own safety, his action had left a painful scar on the soul of the young boy.

One day Nicolas took his problem to his uncle, Bishop Lucas Watzelrode.

"Do you think I am safe in expressing my ideas in public?" he asked.

"I am afraid not, Nicolas," replied his uncle. "Follow the accepted ideas if you want to stay out of trouble. That is the only practical way, you know. There is too much suffering in store for those who hold unconventional views."

Nicolas was well aware of the tortures that were being inflicted in order to make people recant. Only recently he had heard of a doctor who was put to death because he had criticized Galen, the ancient Greek physician who was still regarded as the outstanding medical authority of the world. And in the university library he had just come across a law published in Salzburg:

"A forger shall be boiled to death. A perjurer shall have his tongue torn out. A heretic shall be burned to death. An atheist shall be buried alive."

The young student shuddered when his uncle, who seemed to have read his very thoughts, spoke again: "If you express your strange ideas about a moving earth and a stationary sun, you may fall under suspicion as a heretic."

"But what if I'm convinced that I'm right?" persisted Nicolas.

The bishop placed an affectionate arm around his nephew's shoulders. "The only thing you can be sure of, Nicolas, is that once you are suspected, there is little hope for escape. You know what they say, don't you? 'If you are guilty, you are hanged; if you are innocent, you are drowned.' "

The adage was a familiar one and it referred to the "water test" for persons accused of being witches. These persons were thrown into the water. If they remained afloat, it was taken as a sign that the Devil was helping them—thus they were guilty, taken out of the water and hanged. If they drowned, it was a sign that they were innocent, and their dead bodies were officially freed of the charge.

Nicolas looked at his uncle in perplexity. "What would you advise me to do, Uncle?"

"For the present, keep your mouth shut."

"But that would be cowardly!" cried Nicolas.

"I'm not so sure," said his uncle. "What do you accomplish by exposing yourself to death with your half-formed ideas? What would you leave behind? Nothing but the picture of a fool who would soon be forgotten. Alive, you can do a great deal of good in the world as a scholar, a doctor, a priest—perhaps in all three of these capacities. Meanwhile, study and verify your ideas on astronomy; and later on, if you are certain that you are right, you can present your ideas to the world. Perhaps men will be wiser then and more ready to listen to the truth."

Nicolas followed his uncle's advice. He kept his thoughts more to himself, studied his textbooks by day and the heavens by night and prepared himself for a useful life. His uncle kept urging him to dedicate himself to the Church, and, toward the end of his second year at Kraków, an opening seemed to present itself at Frauenburg, the cathedral over which Bishop Watzelrode presided. One of the canons had just died, and the bishop nominated his nephew to fill the vacancy.

"But I am too young for the job. I haven't even received my degree at the university."

"Nonsense, my boy! There's no such thing as too young. In Italy, as you know, a lad of fourteen was made a cardinal. You're old enough and educated enough to assume the duties of a canon."

Reluctantly Nicolas consented to his uncle's plan, and was relieved when the Pope appointed somebody else to the post. He felt that his studies, far from being ended, had just begun. His interest in medicine had increased, but the curriculum at Kraków was inadequate and he contemplated the idea of attending another university.

He had heard of several good medical schools through his conversations with some of the foreign students at the University of Kraków. One of them, Carlo Poggia, was especially enthusiastic about the intellectual activities of his native country. "Next year I am returning to Bologna," he said, "where I shall complete my studies at the university. Why don't you come along with me?"

The idea intrigued Nicolas. The more his friend spoke about Italy, the more he felt drawn toward it.

"The very air," said Poggia, "expands the imagination and sets it sailing over wide horizons. Some of the finest intellects in the world have settled in Italy. Our country seems to have entered upon a rebirth of learning—a springtime reawakening of the mind."

"I think I shall go with you," said Nicolas, excited over the prospect of new lands and new thoughts.

At the end of the academic school year he returned to Toruń to prepare himself for the journey. His uncle, who had also studied at Bologna, promised to supply him with the necessary funds. The bishop was a rich man and could well afford the money. Throughout his life, Nicolas was free of economic insecurity. He was a rare specimen among men of genius—he always had plenty of money in his purse.

During his vacation at Torún, Nicolas studied Italian. Knowledge of the language, however, was not absolutely necessary, for Latin was the universal language. Many students, in their desire to join the world-wide fraternity of learning, Latinized their names. In keeping with this general practice, Nicolas changed his own last name from Koppernig to Copernicus, the name he used throughout the rest of his life.

Chapter 4

COPERNICUS AND POGGIA started for Bologna in the autumn of 1496, selecting the route through Germany and over the Alps across the Brenner Pass. At Nürnberg he stopped to visit Bernard Walther, a well-known maker of the few astronomical instruments that were in use at that time. Since he was unknown to Walther, Copernicus did not hesitate to speak freely about his ideas on astronomy. He mentioned his doubts about the earth-centered system of Ptolemy.

"The Ptolemaic theory doesn't make sense to me," he said. "According to that theory, the planets move, not steadily, but erratically over the heavens. I've made a number of mathematical calculations on this matter, with Ptolemy as my guide, and the answers always come out wrong."

"This is very interesting," said Bernard Walther. "Go on."

"My studies in the field," continued Copernicus, "are still new. There's much yet to be done. But I have already discovered, I believe, that Ptolemy was in error when he declared that the planet Mars, for example, interrupts its forward motion at times in order to move backward."

"I, too, have noticed this."

"Yes, Herr Walther. Ptolemy was obliged to accept this seemingly retrograde motion of the planets because he insisted upon keeping the earth fixed in the center."

Bernard Walther nodded but said nothing.

"On the other hand," continued Nicolas, "if we assume that the earth is not fixed but moves together with the other planets around the sun, we can account for all their motions in a simple, regular and intelligible pattern over the sky."

"What you say," remarked Walther, "appears to make good sense. Yet if I were you, my friend, I would not be

41

too outspoken on this point. Remember that you are attacking not only a very old idea but a very strong prejudice. You are aiming a death blow at one of mankind's most revered idols."

"What do you mean, Herr Walther?"

"I mean man's image of himself as the king of the universe, seated upon the earth as the central throne, around which the sun and the stars revolve in eternal adoration."

"But Herr Walther——"

"Just wait a minute, young man. I am not through yet. Suppose you are right in your idea. Do you think the world will accept it? Not for generations, I'm afraid—if ever. Your theory would reduce us from a race of kings who live in the capital of the universe to a swarm of insignificant creatures that whirl on a little speck of dust along with the other planets around the sun. You are playing a dangerous game, my boy, for you are planning the greatest revolution in history—a complete overturn in human thought."

"But, Herr Walther, if I *am* right, will not man rise rather than fall through his new knowledge?"

"Just how, my boy?"

"It's hard to explain, sir, but let me tell you how I feel about it. Knowledge makes us free. It liberates us from the shackles of self-conceit and sets our minds in motion. A new and true concept of the universe may shrink our picture of the earth and our own dignity along with it, but it will expand our imagination, permit it to travel into the infinite mystery of space."

"Noble thought, my boy. Nevertheless, I still advise you to keep it to yourself for a long, long time."

As Copernicus continued his journey toward Italy, he thought a great deal about his conversations with Celtes, his uncle and Bernard Walther. Each of them had warned him that it was dangerous to think, or at least to tell the world what you thought. He recalled the fate of Isaiah, of Socrates, of the Christian martyrs—all dedicated men who had died for their beliefs. On the other hand, he remembered the advice of his uncle. Perhaps it was better to choose a life of good works rather than a martyr's death. Well, he was still young, and his thoughts on astronomy were far from complete. He had plenty of time to decide.

As he approached the Alps with their dizzy precipices, towering peaks and cloud-trimmed turbans of snow, his wonder grew at the mystery and the grandeur of the world. One day the narrow ribbon of road skirted a drop of several thousand feet. He looked over the side into the yawning chasm and caught his breath. A single misstep and he would plunge to his death. He had to keep his eyes on the ground for the rest of the time. Yet the higher he climbed, the wider became the sweep of his mental horizon. And at night, when they stopped at an inn on a mountainside, the stars seemed so near that he felt he could almost touch them with his fingertips.

He spoke to Poggia about the mixed feeling of littleness and greatness that the mountains had aroused within him. "It makes me realize how closely our bodies are bound to the earth and how freely our minds could journey among the stars."

"Wait till you get to Italy," said Poggia, his eyes glowing. "You will really know what it means to set your mind on the wing!"

Shortly after their arrival in Bologna, Copernicus realized the truth of Poggia's words. All Italy was a garden filled with marble palaces, exquisite statues, glorious paintings and lofty thoughts. The world at that time was going through one of the flowering periods of history known as the Renaissance, and Italy seemed to have become the very heart of this movement. The memory of Lorenzo the Magnificent was still fresh in the minds of the people, although this banker-patron of art and poetry had died shortly before Copernicus' arrival. And Lorenzo was not the only interesting topic for conversation in Italy. Many people were discussing Botticelli's "Birth of Venus"; the paintings and the sculptures of the amazing young genius Michelangelo; and the works of that virtuoso of all arts and sciences, Leonardo da Vinci.

People referred to Leonardo as *l'uomo universale,* "the universal man," because, as they declared, "there is no subject under the sun in which he is not supreme." Only in Italy, they insisted, could such a man arise.

But what especially intrigued Copernicus was the presence of so many scholars in Bologna. These included not only Italians but other men of genius who had been attracted to the university from all over the world. Among them was a Greek professor by the name of Spyros Soteres, one of the many teachers who had escaped from Constantinople after its capture by the Turks. Like many of the other refugees from that city, Professor Soteres had brought to Italy a number of ancient Greek manuscripts that had remained forgotten for many centuries. Thus the wisdom of Greece was added to the glory of Italy. Copernicus enrolled as a student of Greek under Professor Soteres, and before long he was able to read the astronomical works of Ptolemy in the original language. "In itself, it's a brilliant work," he said to himself, "but, for me, it still fails to make sense."

Nicolas' studies were not confined to Greek and astronomy. He took a number of courses in church law—for he still planned to get a position as a canon—and in medicine. His future career was beginning to take definite shape. He had decided to serve as a canon in order to minister to the spiritual needs of his people, and as a

45

physician to look after their physical welfare. In addition, he hoped to be able to devote his free time to the
study of the Ptolemaic system of astronomy and to check
that system against his own observations of the planets
and the stars.

It was not a matter of all study and no play. Filled
with the exuberance of youth, Copernicus threw himself
into the carnival spirit of the Italian Renaissance. He
abandoned the formal cap and gown that he had worn at
the University of Kraków, and chose instead the finery
worn by the wealthier students at Bologna. He flushed
with a sense of mingled bashfulness and pride when he
looked into the mirror and saw himself arrayed in his
new outfit for the first time. For a while he stood gazing
at his handsome reflection, his lips parted in a shy smile,
and turned away from the mirror only when he heard a
knock on the door. In answer to his call, Carlo Poggia entered the room.

"What have we here?" he cried. "A Polish priest transformed into an Italian nobleman! Or, should I say,
Apollo descended from Mount Olympus and dressed in
the latest Bolognese fashion!"

"Please don't embarrass me," said Nicolas, laughing
nervously.

"Why should you be embarrassed? The clothes look
very well on you." Poggia gazed with exaggerated inter-

est at his friend's sapphire-blue jacket with its puffed yellow sleeves and red velvet cuffs. He nodded his head in approval of the sky-blue tights, the cherry-red beret, with nodding plume, and the matching red slippers.

"Stop staring, Carlo, and tell me what you've come for."

Poggia could not resist teasing Copernicus a little longer.

"All in good time, Niccolò mio, but first let me admire you. If I had those legs of yours, I'd have all the beautiful girls in the city pursuing me! You're so impressive, from head to toe, I think I shall call you 'Niccolò the Magnificent' from now on!"

Copernicus pulled off his beret, frowning at the plume as he did so. "If you're through with your nonsense, tell me what's on your mind."

"Very little as a rule, Nicolas, as you well know—but just now I have news that will interest you. Fra Girolamo is coming to preach at Bologna."

This news was indeed interesting. Everybody in Italy was talking about Girolamo Savonarola. Professor Soteres had heard his "inspired" preaching at Florence. "That man," he had told Copernicus, "is a flame in the wind. He sets every mind ablaze with the ardor of his words. When you listen to him, you become a violent partisan—either for or against him."

47

Copernicus was familiar with the story of this dynamic religious leader. Starting life as a physician, Savonarola had abandoned his medical practice to become a Dominican friar. The world, he declared, suffered much more grievously from its spiritual than from its physical diseases. He escaped from society, as he wrote his father, in order to find peace for himself. But he did not allow society to escape from the lashings of his tongue. He upbraided the kings for their tyranny and the aristocrats for their luxury. He spoke out passionately for the poor, whom he called "the little people." And he claimed to be "the chosen Voice of God," directed to regenerate the world.

He had started his preaching at the Monastery of Bologna. Later he had moved to the Convent of San Marco in Florence. Now he was coming back to speak to the people of Bologna. "He isn't much to look at," Professor Soteres told Copernicus, "but he carries you away with him the moment he starts to speak."

Copernicus could hardly wait to hear this modern prophet. "Here," he said to himself, "is a man who dares to speak his thoughts freely and who thus far has not been punished for his ideas." Savonarola might well serve as an inspiration.

In the meantime his life at Bologna had received a new spur. Following the custom of his student days at Kra-

ków, he took frequent walks through the streets and stopped to converse with all sorts of people. Carlo Poggia, his usual companion on these walks, pointed out the beauties of the quaint city, with its winding streets, turreted castles and miles upon miles of outdoor shops where the goods were protected from the weather under vaulted colonnades. "These colonnades," explained Poggia, "are the product of our Italian fondness for living in the open air. Our Bolognese houses are generally built with overhanging walls in the upper stories."

Copernicus nodded. "Yes, I have noticed that peculiarity. These open shops, displaying their colors from within their shelters, give you the impression that you are walking through an endless art museum."

Indeed, the entire city was like a gallery of living pictures. Strollers in their gay costumes, peddlers with their baskets of gewgaws, traders hawking their wares with strident voices, women carrying their babies wrapped up like mummies on their backs, peasants driving mule carts loaded with fruits and vegetables—all jostled one another and filled the narrow streets. Now and then, as the two friends sauntered along the streets, they were unceremoniously separated by an intruder—one of the numerous pigs that were allowed to roam freely throughout the city. Bologna, like many of the other cities at that period, was a place of beautiful sights and ugly smells.

There were also occasional sounds that struck terror into the hearts of the people. One day Copernicus and his brother Andreas, who had joined him as a student at Bologna, took a stroll out into the country. Suddenly they heard the tinkling of a bell. It was the warning voice of a leper—a signal for all those in the vicinity to avoid his polluted presence.

Andreas, who was extremely sensitive, shuddered at the sound. "The very thought of a leper," he whispered, "sends a shiver down my spine!"

Nicolas tried to reassure him. "Do not be afraid, Andreas. The poor man needs to be pitied rather than shunned."

His brother shook his head. "I'm leaving. The whole atmosphere around here must be tainted with his disease!"

Nicolas tried once more to calm Andreas' fears. "Don't you remember the story of Saint Francis? He once met a leper on the roadside, but instead of turning away, he ran forward and embraced him as a brother in distress. Yet nothing happened to Saint Francis. I shall go up to this sick man and give him alms."

"Do as you like, Nicolas," insisted Andreas. "As for me, you'll find me at our rooms when you get back." Turning on his heel, he hurried away from the sound of the bell.

It was fortunate that Andreas was unable to glimpse into the future and realize that before long he himself would need to be pitied rather than shunned.

For the time being, however, life at Bologna went on at a carefree pace. The two brothers were welcome guests at frequent parties held in the aristocratic homes of the city. They attended the mass meetings of the students, who proposed the laws for the government of the university. They voted in the elections of the rector, or governor, who served two years as the supreme head of the institution. They joined in the petitions of the student body to get higher salaries for their professors, for the teaching profession was woefully underpaid.

One of the measures for securing additional money for the faculty was a rather unusual custom to which the students resorted regularly on the rector's election day. Immediately after the election the students tore off the successful candidate's garments, ripping them to pieces and selling the "relics" to the wealthy townsmen at exorbitant prices. "The Rector's pain," they chanted, "is the Teachers' gain."

These diversions took but a small part of Copernicus' time. On the whole, his working hours were long and strenuous. His classes began at seven in the morning and lasted till seven in the evening. Frequently he attended additional lectures and sermons delivered by the famous scholars who visited Bologna.

One of these notable occasions was the address that Savonarola was to give at Bologna. Since the university auditorium was too small to accommodate the vast audience that clamored to hear him, the spacious monastery had been selected for the purpose. The atmosphere was noticeably charged with emotion by the time Savonarola arrived. Every available inch of space in the auditorium had been filled. People craned forward for a first glimpse of the boyish-looking monk in a white surplice as he approached the pulpit.

"There he is!" Professor Soteres whispered excitedly to Nicolas.

Copernicus could hardly believe his eyes. This pale, puny fellow, with narrow shoulders, sunken cheeks and protruding lower lip like that of a child trembling on the verge of tears—could this be the dynamic power that had shaken the thrones of the world?

Looking fragile and ailing, Savonarola moved slowly across the pulpit and stopped behind the lectern, which concealed most of his body. Only his head and shoulders were visible above the top. Then, for the first time, his energy began to flame up through his eyes. Deep-set under their red bushy brows, they were like torches that burned from within, seeming to pierce the entire auditorium with an almost unearthly glow. As soon as he began to speak, the audience was transformed into a single instrument that vibrated under his magical skill. They laughed, wept, screamed and swayed to the rhythm of his words.

"I abhor tyranny," he cried, "and I adore freedom! I pity the rich for their arrogance, and the poor for their humility. I have come to build a new world in which there shall be neither rich nor poor!"

Then he told his audience how he had organized a number of banks to lend money to the poor without interest. "My purpose," he said, "is to establish the Kingdom of God on earth."

After this introduction he launched into a diatribe against the institutions that hampered the building of this Kingdom. Copernicus was especially impressed by Savonarola's denunciation of astrology, which the prophet called the root of all godlessness and superstition and vice. "Astrology," he declared, "is the pseudo-knowledge of the ignorant who falsely believe that a man's fortune depends upon the position of the stars at the time of his birth. But I tell you that a man's fortune depends upon his faith in God and his love toward his fellow men. A man is ill starred because he is ill disposed, not because he has been born under a so-called 'unlucky' star."

53

Savonarola, felt Copernicus, was a man after his own heart. "And the authorities are leaving *him* alone!" This thought kept ringing like a refrain in the mind of the Polish student. "It *is* safe to think for yourself and to express your thoughts to the world!"

Savonarola had now reached the climax of his sermon. "The scourge of God," he cried, "is at our very doors. The barbarians are already on their way across the Alps to burn, ravage and kill. They will lead you into captivity like bears, with iron rings through your noses. In vain you will seek to flee to the right and to the left—the scourge of God will appear on every side; on every side there will be darkness. You will find no place to hide your heads. Darkness here, darkness there, all the world in tumult, earth and heaven, sun and moon—all creation swallowed up in the blackness of the night!" A wave of terror swept over the audience as he thundered out his denunciations. And then, suddenly, his voice changed to a cry of compassion as he lifted his arms to the sky and prayed: "Mercy, O God! Mercy in the name of Christ!"

After he finished speaking, several of the audience rushed up to the pulpit and wailed, "Save us, Fra Girolamo! Deliver us from the wrath of the Lord!"

"Give to the poor," he shouted above the uproar, "and you shall be saved!"

At these words there was a general surge toward the

speaker. Men whipped open their leather purses and tossed gold and silver coins at his feet. Women stripped off their rings and necklaces and bracelets and heaped them upon a mounting pile. The daughter of one of the leading bankers of Bologna tore off her silk mantle, all the while shouting hysterically, "No more rich garments for me! From now on I live for the poor!"

Never had Copernicus witnessed such a scene. And even he, though the blood of a colder climate flowed in his veins, was moved almost to the point of adoration. Later on, when the clamor had somewhat subsided, he went to the clerk who had been assigned to record the speech, and asked for a copy. Much to his surprise, there was no complete speech available. "I had to stop writing several times," the clerk explained. "The tears so blurred my eyes that I couldn't see to write."

As soon as Savonarola returned to the monastery cell where he was staying during his visit to Bologna, Copernicus called on him. He found the preacher slumped down in a chair, his face resting in the palms of his hands.

Savonarola looked up at his visitor's greeting. Copernicus was deeply moved at the change that had taken place in the man who only a few minutes ago had hurled his thunderbolts at the world. He looked pale and tired and sick now—a pathetic child who desperately needed his Father's care.

Savonarola was the first to speak. "I can read your thoughts, young man. You are surprised at my appearance. Am I right?"

Copernicus could only blurt out a few incoherent words: "I didn't know . . . couldn't imagine . . ."

"I understand, my son. When I preach, an inner fire burns at my bones and illumines the world. But when I get through, the fire dies down and only the ashes remain."

Loath to impose upon the man who was so obviously in need of rest, Copernicus was about to withdraw, but Savonarola urged him to stay. Nicolas spoke first about his admiration for the priest's courage; then he opened his own heart. He explained his contempt for the stupidities and superstitions of astrology, and spoke of his revolutionary ideas, still vague in his own mind, concerning the motions of the heavenly bodies.

"The final proof of my ideas," he concluded, "will require many years of study. But I have to discuss them with people of learning, for it is only through discussion that we can arrive at the truth. Do you agree with me, Fra Girolamo?"

"My son, I both agree and disagree. First let me tell you why I disagree. I feel that the world does not need

new ideas. What it needs is an honest return to the old—
the old beliefs of the Prophets, the Apostles, the followers of Moses and Isaiah and Christ—the simple formula
of compassion and love. But your new ideas are likely
to bring confusion instead of peace into the world."

"You are speaking, Fra Girolamo, about the field of
human conduct—the way people ought to act toward
one another. And I am sure you are right. There can
never be any discovery greater than the Golden Rule:
'Do unto others as you would have them do unto you.'
But may I venture to suggest that my work is in a somewhat different field—*scientific knowledge*. In this field
there are always new discoveries, and each discovery is a
forward step toward our true understanding of God."

"I shall not argue with you about that, my son. I have
but little interest in science. However, let me point out
wherein I agree with you. Speak up whenever you feel
convinced that you are right. I have been doing this all
my life, and thus far no harm has come to me."

At these words Copernicus approached Savonarola
and impulsively clasped his small, slender hands between his own. "Thank you, Fra Girolamo," he cried
fervently. "You have given me a light to guide me from
now on!"

"Don't misunderstand me, my son," smiled the older
man—rather wistfully, it seemed to Copernicus. "I do

not speak out just because I am safe. I am determined to proclaim the truth even at the cost of my life. But I have not yet been molested, and I hope I shall remain unmolested to the end."

Copernicus left the monastery with a new resolve. Henceforward, he intended to discuss his views openly. And, like Fra Girolamo, he hoped to find it safe to speak the truth. Perhaps he would be allowed to express his scientific ideas, just as Savonarola was proclaiming his religious convictions, without interference from the ruling powers of the world. Apparently his former advisers were wrong. Professor Celtes, Uncle Watzelrode and Herr Walther had perhaps unwisely sealed his lips. He would no longer remain silent.

He began to discuss his doubts about the Ptolemaic system with some of the more liberal teachers at the university, especially with Domenico da Novara, a professor of astronomy. Together they began to study the heavens and calculate the positions of the planets and stars at various times. Their observations and calculations showed them that the celestial revolutions could not be fitted into the Ptolemaic plan. According to Ptolemy, the planets were supposed to enter into an entirely different circular path each day. "It would be altogether unworthy of the sublime Creator," observed Copernicus, "to have moved all these planets according to different rules, and to have created the universe to resemble a monster senselessly patched together from the bodies of many diverse creatures. I am determined to get at the truth of this matter before I am through. I am determined to find, if at all possible, one law to explain the motions of all the heavenly spheres."

The young astronomer experienced a brief period of exaltation, during which he felt stimulated, afire with the spirit of an intrepid explorer and, like Savonarola, free.

And then came a sudden blow. Fra Girolamo was arrested for speaking out against the ruling authorities. Shortly afterward came the news of his trial, condemnation and death. In the month of May, 1498, Girolamo Savonarola was stoned, hanged and then burned in the Piazza della Signoria in Florence.

Copernicus was forced once more to accept the fact that it was not wise to express doubts or unconventional theories and new ideas. He was learning that the road to courage is as steep and long as the way to the stars.

Chapter 5

BEFORE COPERNICUS received his degree at the University of Bologna, there was another vacancy in Lucas Watzelrode's diocese, and this time the bishop succeeded in having him appointed to the post. Nicolas did not immediately assume his canonical duties at the cathedral, although he came back to Frauenburg briefly to be officially installed in office. He was granted further leave of absence to continue his studies, and he returned to Italy.

In 1500 Nicolas was sent to Rome as a special legate to attend the Jubilee celebration of the Catholic Church that marked the beginning of the sixteenth century. Copernicus welcomed the opportunity to visit the Eternal City—and he was not the only one. Some of the greatest minds of Europe flocked to Rome for the "marriage of Classical and Christian culture"—the ideas of the old world and the ideals of the new. In that great Jubilee Year Nicolas met Erasmus, the priest who had become inactive in the Church in order to address himself to the world. And Reuchlin, the Humanist who had brought his interpretation of the Old Testament for the enlightenment of the New. Here, too, Nicolas became acquainted with a number of other Humanists, the teachers who tried to graft the wisdom of ancient learning upon the tree of Christian faith.

Urged by some of these Humanists, Copernicus delivered a number of lectures in Rome, but he took care to say little about his astronomical studies. He did, however, mention an eclipse of the moon that he had observed in Rome: "And during that eclipse, I noticed that the shadow of the earth was circular. This would seem to indicate that the earth is a sphere."

There was a gasp from a few members of the audience at this unorthodox idea, but most of the listeners nodded in agreement. Since the voyages of Columbus, it was generally accepted in learned circles that the earth was round. Copernicus noted with satisfaction that his remarks about the earth's spherical shadow on the moon had created so little commotion. Perhaps his other ideas, too, would find a favorable reception when he was ready to submit them to the world.

One evening, at a reception of scholars and artists held at the house of one of the cardinals, he met Michelangelo, who, like Copernicus, had come to Rome for the Jubilee. When Nicolas was introduced to the young Florentine painter, he was taken somewhat aback, for Michelangelo hardly looked like an artist. His short, tumbled hair fell untidily over his face, which was disfigured by a sprawling nose flattened at the bridge. He smiled when he saw Nicolas' quizzical look.

"My nose," he explained, "is my broken badge—not of courage but of timidity."

Copernicus was too polite to give voice to his curiosity, so he said nothing. Michelangelo, however, was more than willing to speak. He had taken a fancy to Copernicus.

"It was broken in a fight that was not of my choosing," he said. "Here is how it happened: One day, as I was carving out the statue of an old man in the garden of Lorenzo the Magnificent, Messer Lorenzo himself happened to come by. He looked at my work and then turned to me. 'My boy,' he said, 'don't you know that an old man must have lost some of his teeth?'

" 'Yes, Signor,' I replied. And, seizing a hammer, I knocked out a couple of teeth in the face of the statue."

"But," said Copernicus, "what has all this got to do with your nose?"

"I'm just coming to it, my friend. One of my fellow apprentices at Lorenzo's palace, the quick-tempered and strong-fisted Torrigiano, was jealous over the attention paid to me by our patron. As soon as Torrigiano and I were left alone, he rushed up to me and shouted, 'Let's see what a couple of missing teeth will do to *your* face!'

"As he swung his fist, I ducked and received the full blow on the bridge of my nose."

"What a tragedy!" exclaimed Nicolas with a look of genuine distress in his eyes.

"But I was lucky after all. The blow might have killed me. Indeed, they carried me home for dead. As it is, I am merely disfigured for life."

Copernicus and Michelangelo became close friends and spent many hours together during the Jubilee. Though generally uncommunicative with others—because he was sensitive about his distorted face—the Italian artist opened his heart to his Polish companion. He told Copernicus about his hopes and plans, and Copernicus in turn told Michelangelo about his imaginary excursions into the skies. Both of them shared a common interest—the teaching of Savonarola. One of Michelangelo's brothers, inspired by Savonarola, had renounced the world and entered a Dominican monastery.

"I, too," said Michelangelo, "was for a time tempted to abandon my art and become a Dominican monk. My soul was caught up in a terrific struggle between beauty and duty, art and religion, skepticism and faith."

"How then," asked Copernicus, "did you resolve the struggle?"

"By reconciling the two ideas that at first had appeared so contradictory. I decided to dedicate my life to religion *and* art—to reveal the beauty of holiness and the holiness of beauty."

"I know exactly what you mean!" exclaimed Copernicus. "I, too, have gone through a similar struggle—to choose between religion and science. And, like yourself, I have decided to devote my work to the harmonious union of the two—religion *and* science."

"Yes," said Michelangelo, "in this respect you and I are very much alike. We are also alike in another way. Both of us are trying to obtain, if we can, a God's-eye view of the world. It is my ambition to paint angels and men against the background of eternity; your ambition is to give to the world a true vision of that background."

Easter Sunday climaxed the festivities of the Jubilee. A procession, which began with the ringing of the church bells at sunrise, lasted throughout the entire day. The sky was a vast blue tent overhead. Michelangelo and Copernicus stood on the balcony of a house overlooking Saint Anne's Gate and watched the pageant streaming toward the Vatican for the blessing of Pope Alexander VI. It seemed as if all Europe had congregated in the Holy City for the historic occasion. Both the scientist and the artist were thrilled at the spectacle as the history of the Holy City unfolded before their eyes. Nobles rolled by in carriages decorated with the figures of saints and martyrs; warriors pranced by on horses caparisoned in silver and gold; ladies were dazzling in fabulous jewels and furred mantles; long columns of acolytes bore lighted tapers and blazing torches. Scholars, bankers, tradesmen, artisans, apprentices, *popolani,* or middle-class citizens, priests and peasants formed an endless procession through the streets of the city, following an image of the Lord held aloft on a platform. A billow of laces created the impression of God riding on a chariot of clouds.

On that day Rome—which ordinarily held less than seventy thousand souls—was filled with a throng of two hundred thousand people who had come from everywhere to compose their differences and to kneel before the Pope as a symbol of harmony under the banner of Christ.

Yet Rome was far from a harmonious city at that period. Copernicus, who remained there for a year, learned that it was a place of strange contrasts—a mixture of art and artificiality, prayer and poison, courage and cruelty, learning and lust. It was during his stay in Rome that the city was rocked by the conviction and hanging of one of Italy's leading physicians—a grasping hypocrite who had supplemented his healing with robbery and murder. Copernicus was glad that he had chosen a career in the Church. From that vantage point he hoped he might be able to bring a little of the wisdom of God to the foolishness of men.

And, too, he hoped to help them in their misery. During his Roman visit he witnessed the terrors of a plague. In the sixteenth century, these dread epidemics were almost as frequent as the changing of the seasons. Amid all the horror and filth, Copernicus was deeply moved to find some of the richest ladies of the city moving about the streets, tending the sick and feeding children who had lost their parents.

The sight of such great suffering convinced Copernicus that he should go to medical school and learn what he could to save lives and ease pain. He wrote to his uncle, requesting an extended leave of absence, and entered the University of Padua for his medical studies.

He saw new scenes, new faces, everywhere he went—but always the same stars overhead. Whatever he did, his thoughts were never far removed from the heavens. He took along with him his astronomical instruments—he depended almost entirely upon the gnomon for measuring the meridian altitude of the sun and the Jacob's staff for computing the angles of the planets—and he continued to spend as much time as he could watching the skies. He made observations of the positions of the planets in relation to the stars and noted the elevations of the moon above the horizon. Again and again, when he tried to follow the "motions of the sun around the earth"—in accordance with the Ptolemaic system—he found himself caught "like a bird in a cage," as he expressed it. For indeed, the sun, as Ptolemy had claimed, did seem to move in an annual spiral of circles from north to south, and then back again from south to north, enclosing the earth as in a "bird cage of celestial loops." This was a pretty enough concept. But why did the planets perform such peculiar gyrations as they wandered in and out of the sun's spiral cage? This was the question that perplexed Copernicus. Thus far he could find no answer.

His interest in astronomy did not prevent him from pursuing other subjects, and while at Padua he became absorbed in his medical studies. Surgery at that time belonged not to the doctors but to the barbers, and it was considered as degrading for a doctor to perform an operation as to shave a beard. Physiology and anatomy were studied from textbooks rather than demonstrated on the human body. Little was understood about its structure and mechanisms. Now and then the corpse of an executed criminal was dissected at the medical college, but it was the barbers rather than the students who did the dissecting. Occasionally the professor and the students, their delicate sensibilities fortified by generous doses of wine, would attend the dissections. The professor would point out the various organs and the students would take a few notes, but the barbers did all the "ghastly" work.

Doctors of that century knew very little about medicine as we understand it today. They received no clinical experience or hospital training, and instruction was based largely upon the writings of ancient Greek, Latin, Arabic and Hebrew physicians. There was one universal prescription for all illness—prayer. But Copernicus, a devout believer in prayer, was convinced that spiritual remedies were not sufficient to heal the sick. On the other hand, he disavowed charms, amulets, and elaborate concoctions of herbs and plants that some doctors prescribed for their patients. These so-called physicians paid more attention to the phase of the moon when plucking an herb than they did to the healing qualities of the plant itself. Copernicus refused to rely on astrology for treatment and made the criterion for a remedy its effectiveness as a cure.

He became disgusted when he heard of doctors tying a red thread around a man's neck to stop a nose bleed; and thought it equally stupid to prescribe a raw potato to be carried in a pocket to cure rheumatic pains.

His critical attitude toward the practice of medicine led to a repetition of his experiences at other universities. One day he ventured to criticize a lecture on the human body in which the professor tried to prove that there was a mystic relationship between astrology and medicine.

"The human body," the professor said, "is a small-scale model of the universe. Each part of the body corresponds to a sign of the Zodiac. The head is analogous to Aries, the Ram; the feet to Pisces, the Fishes; the eyes to the sun and the moon; and so on. Therefore we must treat every sick part of the body in accordance with the position of its corresponding heavenly body at the time of the sickness. And we must pluck the herbs for the remedy at the precise moment of the night, day or month when the signs of the Zodiac are most favorable for the cure of that particular ailment in that particular part of the body."

The professor then expanded this theory by pointing to a complicated map filled with diagrams of constellations, planets and sections of the human body that crossed and intercrossed in a veritable jungle of incomprehensible stupidity. Copernicus listened with mounting indignation, and at the end of the lecture he approached the professor.

"Don't you think, sir, that it would be a better idea to study the body as a separate science, and to try to heal it without any mystical references to the stars?"

The professor glared at him like a judge passing sentence on a criminal. "Young man," he growled, "you talk like a heretic!" And then, addressing the entire class, he said, "Gentlemen, don't dare to depart from the established principles of the past! To seek the new is to depart from the wisdom of the old!"

"But, sir," Copernicus persisted, "even the old principles were new at the time they were established. All knowledge, I believe, is the result of a continual breaking away from narrower to wider fields. This is true of medicine just as it is true of religion, exploration and art. May I presume to suggest, sir, that even Hippocrates and Galen expounded ideas which, in their own day, were new?"

70

"And may I remind *you,* young man, that to defy Galen today is a crime punishable by imprisonment or even death?"

Realizing that to question Galen was considered as heretical as to question Ptolemy, Copernicus held his peace as he continued his medical studies. Privately dismissing old superstitions and folklore, he began to seek his own approach to the art of healing. His reason told him that he could help his patients more by observing their condition than by speculating on the connection between the signs of the Zodiac and the human body and its ailments.

He left the University of Padua without a medical diploma, perhaps feeling that such a diploma, though it might add prestige, would in no way increase his skill. Moreover, a medical practitioner needed no college degree in the early part of the sixteenth century. Copernicus intended to learn as he went along. The sick among the members of his flock at Frauenburg, who had always been at the mercy of charlatans and quacks, would be grateful for the services of a man who had received some medical training, however inadequate.

Chapter 6

THUS FAR, COPERNICUS had been a scholar without a diploma. He had received no degree either in astronomy or in medicine. Before assuming his canonical duties, however, he felt it advisable to get at least one degree: a Doctorate of Canon Law.

For this purpose he enrolled as a theological student at the University of Ferrara. Here he found less opposition to his ideas than he had encountered at Kraków,

Bologna or Padua. But, on the other hand, he himself offered less opposition to the ideas of his new teachers at Ferrara. Throughout his life Copernicus remained a faithful servant of the Church.

His student days at Ferrara were enlivened by a number of exciting events. In this city of splendid cathedrals, ornate palaces, quarrelsome politicians and nobles, gossip provided entertainment for the lesser citizens. The transgressions of the famous d'Este family could always be depended upon for appetizing tidbits of news. There were no newspapers in those days, but the barber shops served as an excellent substitute for our modern press. Whenever Copernicus went to his barber, Angelo, he heard of another outrageous escapade at the palace d'Estes.

Lucrezia was married to Alfonso d'Este I, son of Ercole! Machiavelli was not a "political adventurer," nor did he have Cesare under his influence. Cesare was a politically ruthless prince who served as Machiavelli's model for *The Prince*.

One of the most talked-about members of the ducal family was Lucrezia Borgia—the young and beautiful but unpopular wife of Alfonso d'Este I. Lucrezia, her brother Duke Cesare Borgia, and the Italian statesman Niccolò Machiavelli were also favorite topics of conversation.

73

"I have been told," Angelo was saying one day, "that Machiavelli is a disciple of the devil. They say he has turned the Ten Commandments upside down. He has caught the ear of Cesare Borgia and has convinced him that a prince's best weapons for maintaining his power are hypocrisy and murder."

"You are quite right in what you have heard," agreed one of Angelo's customers. "I have just come from Romagna, and the entire district is buzzing with ugly rumors about the prince. The other day he embraced a friend whom he had invited to dinner, and stabbed him in the midst of the embrace."

"This," observed another man, "is how he gets rid of all his rivals. A dagger with a kiss, and poison in a cup of wine."

"They say," said Angelo, "that it was Cesare Borgia who helped his sister Lucrezia poison her former husband, the Duke of Bisceglie."

"Yet outwardly," observed Copernicus, "they seem to be God-fearing gentlefolk. I understand they are lavish in their gifts to the Church and famous for their generosity to the poor."

The visitor from Romagna looked at Copernicus and noted his Polish features. "I see you are a stranger in Italy, sir, so you don't understand the ways of our dukes and princes. Their pretended piety is but a veil that

74

hides their hypocrisy. They point toward heaven with one hand and plunder the earth with the other. No wonder the duke has overrun almost the entire territory of Central Italy!"

Copernicus had heard similar scandals about other leading Italian families—the Medicis, the Sforzas, the d'Estes—amazing contradictions of good and evil. Yet he was loath to believe all he had heard, preferring to have proof before he condemned. The Italians he had met personally were kind and wholesome people. Duplicity seemed quite foreign to their national character. Moreover, he had seen Lucrezia Borgia two or three times while she was worshiping at the San Francesco Cathedral. They were momentary glimpses, but they had revealed a face that appeared sensitive and devout. "Perhaps," he ventured to suggest, "all this is mere hearsay. Nobody can actually prove these ugly stories about Cesare Borgia or the Countess d'Este."

The visitor from Romagna looked scornfully at Copernicus. "Do you mind telling me, sir, what your occupation is?"

"I am a canon studying church law at Ferrara. But my chief interest is astronomy."

"Ah, a stargazer," whispered the Florentine to Angelo. "No wonder he doesn't see what's going on under his nose!"

Copernicus enjoyed his contacts with the common people of Italy. They were excitable and argumentative and quick to take offense, but they were equally quick to befriend, and their generosity knew no bounds. Quite unscrupulous, however, were the ruling classes of the Italian cities, in spite of Copernicus' unwillingness to believe rumors and gossip.

"Our entire nobility," a writer observed at the time, "is a syndicate of murder." There was hardly a palace without its hired assassins. War was the favorite pastime of the day. The masses were as lambs led to the slaughter; and the best paintings and statues in the galleries were at the mercy of the soldiers. A few years earlier the French bowmen who had invaded Milan used Leonardo da Vinci's equestrian statue of Francesco Sforza as a target for their archery. As a result of the vandalism, a masterpiece regarded as the Eighth Wonder of the World was lost for all time.

Copernicus was thankful that his own destiny had turned him away from military ambitions. It was good to have dedicated his life to the service of God and the contemplation of the stars.

After ten years of study and travel in various cities of Italy, Copernicus received his doctorate at Ferrara. The graduation, like most traditional ceremonies of the period, was an imposing and picturesque event—as well as a very costly experience for the candidates. At the end of the exercises, which concluded with a public address by the new "Doctor of Canon Law," the entire audience —students, faculty and dignitaries of the town—were invited to a banquet at the doctor's expense. It was fortunate that Copernicus could afford this luxury. Many a deserving student was unable to obtain his doctorate because he lacked the funds for this public entertainment.

Even Copernicus, who was comparatively well to do, sank most of his savings into the mountains of macaroni, boiled kid, spiced game, capon and partridge served with the feathers on. There was a free flow of wine and conversation at the table. Copernicus was opposed to excessive self-denial or excessive self-indulgence. However, his extravagance for this entertainment was expected of a student whose uncle was a wealthy bishop and who himself was coming into a position of such great promise. As far as he was concerned, this was the final splurge of his career, and he determined to live more in keeping with his own simple tastes.

Chapter 7

In 1506 Copernicus returned to Frauenburg, a Baltic seaport and capital of the Polish diocese of Ermland, to begin his official duties as canon at the cathedral.

There were at Frauenburg sixteen church officers who served as political as well as religious administrators of the district, an area of over twenty-five square miles. They presided as judges, leased the farms to the peasants, collected the rents, appointed the magistrates and determined the taxes for the hunting and fishing rights.

Copernicus was now financially independent. Like all the other canons of that period, he was given two servants and three horses for his personal use. In addition to his free residence on Cathedral Hill, he received a farm whose total income became his private property. It was the beginning of the happiest period in the life of Copernicus. His religious duties, as compared to his civil responsibilities, were rather light. He had to observe his morning and evening devotions, read the masses, preside at the death anniversaries of the important people of the district and attend the meetings of the ecclesiastical council. Shortly after his return, however, his uncle released him from those duties and installed him as his physician at Heilsberg Castle, about forty miles inland from Frauenburg. Here Lucas Watzelrode lived in royal splendor, not only as head of the Frauenburg Cathedral, but also as the ruler of Ermland.

A long and bitter struggle between the Polish rulers of Ermland and the Teutonic Knights had often subjected Heilsberg Castle to the ravages of fire and sword. The latest attack against the castle had taken place only a few years earlier when Copernicus was a student at Bologna. The castle had been partly destroyed and several of its defenders had lost their lives, but the attack had been repulsed and Bishop Watzelrode had rebuilt the castle and fortified it against future assaults.

For the present, things were quiet. "But," the bishop warned Nicolas, "we must always be on the alert. One can never tell when the wolves may next descend upon our flock."

Copernicus smiled grimly to himself when he learned about the turbulent state of affairs at Heilsberg. He had chosen a clerical life in order to live in peace, but it seemed that he was destined to a stormy career against his will. "While there's life, there's strife," he said to his uncle, repeating an old Polish adage.

The bishop nodded in solemn agreement, then smiled. "At any rate, let's try our best to stay alive. And that is part of your business, Nicolas—to keep your old uncle's skin and bones together. I understand the Teutonic Order is praying daily for my death."

The bishop's joke was somewhat forced. In addition to his advanced years, feeble health and continual struggle against the Teutonic Order, he had also incurred the displeasure of King Sigismund I. The people of Ermland wanted their state to be free and independent; they resented the rule of the Polish king no less than that of the Teutonic Knights. And between the anger of King Sigismund and the threats of the Order, the bishop's declining years were full of tension and worry. But the presence of his nephew brought him a measure of joy. The quiet cheerfulness of Copernicus served as a balm to his troubled soul, and the knowledge that he had a physician in his castle allayed his fear of illness.

Copernicus served his uncle in another important capacity—as intermediary between him and the king. Bishop Watzelrode sent him on a number of diplomatic missions to King Sigismund, and Copernicus' open face and honest words made a favorable impression upon the monarch. "With a man like you in the bishop's council," said Sigismund, "I believe there will be peace between Poland and Ermland."

"I am grateful to your Majesty for thinking so kindly of me," replied Copernicus. "As your Majesty knows, my life is dedicated to the service of our Lord—the Prince of Peace."

Copernicus remained at Heilsberg from 1506 to 1512. As busy as he was with various duties at the castle, he managed to find time for the interest that lay closest to his heart. During those years he began to outline his revolutionary ideas about astronomy.

It was a long, painstaking task he set himself. Since there were no telescopes in those days, the eye was practically the only instrument that could observe the stars— and their complicated revolutions in the heavens were too distant and too faint to be checked by the naked eye.

Copernicus had to take careful mathematical measurements of the positions of the stars at certain times in order to develop his new theory accurately. The mathematics that Copernicus had taken while a student enabled him to make the necessary calculations.

The more he studied and observed the heavens, the more he was convinced that it could all be reduced to a few simple laws—or perhaps a single law that could explain the successions of days and nights, the revolutions of the seasons, the eclipses of the sun and the moon, the reappearance of the stars at their appointed time through the centuries. It was his intention to try and establish the "heliocentric law"—the principle of a universe with a central sun around which all the planets revolve.

Copernicus began writing a pamphlet entitled *The Little Commentary*, a short account of his own theories. "The ideas I am trying to advance," he explained to his uncle, "are not my own. I have merely done a great deal of reading and thinking and have woven various pieces of information together. Let me briefly recall these threads which I am trying to weave into one theory. The progress of our astronomical knowledge may be traced as a journey from our senses, through our imagination, to our mind."

"It sounds like a fascinating journey," said the bishop. "Go on, please, and I shall be glad to follow."

"The earliest astronomers," Copernicus went on, "relied entirely upon their senses. They believed only what they saw—the earth surrounded by oceans, rising into mountains, and topped by a circular sky which was lighted by the lamps of the sun and the moon and the stars. This is how they pictured the universe: they looked upon the earth as a round island in the center; the sky was a solid firmament, or vaulted ceiling, supported by a range of mountains that encircled the world beyond the seas."

"It's an interesting picture. Go on."

"Later, human imagination came into play as an aid to the senses. The stars appeared to be grouped into fantastic figures resembling animals and men. And so the astronomers invented names for these groups. They called them 'Cancer,' the Constellation of the Crab; 'Capricorn,' the Constellation of the Goat; 'Pisces,' the Star Group of the Fishes; 'Gemini,' 'Hercules,' 'Orion,' 'Perseus' and so on."

His uncle nodded. "And this is how the pseudoscience of astrology arose. People imagined that if the constellations resembled the figures of men and animals on earth, they must therefore exert an influence upon all living creatures."

"Yes," replied Copernicus, "but we should not belittle their contribution to our general knowledge. We can find many gems of truth concealed in the rubbish of their errors. Our senses and our flights of imagination may carry us well along the highway to truth. But in the end we must turn to our reasoning faculty, supported by our mathematical knowledge, as our infallible guide."

Copernicus paused for a moment and then went on: "At first, then, our ideas about the world were based upon imaginative speculation. We know that the Babylonians and Egyptians made observations and recorded them. Next came a period of scientific investigation, begun by the Greeks. They were the first to make any *theoretical* contributions to astronomy. The Greek philosophers and scientists were eager to take the world apart and put it together again."

"But their ideas about astronomy were primitive, weren't they?"

"In some ways, yes. Don't forget that they were just beginning a new and intricate field of investigation. All beginnings are rather crude. Nevertheless, I am indebted to the ancient Greeks for most of my ideas. It was the Greek Pythagoras who first declared that the earth is a sphere floating in space. And it was another Greek, Philolaus, who expressed the view that the center of the universe is not the earth but a celestial fire around

84

which the earth revolves in a daily circle. He made a mistake, however, in supposing that the sun as well as the earth revolves around the central fire."

"But the ideas of Pythagoras and Philolaus were soon forgotten," observed the bishop.

"Yes," Copernicus agreed. "Having no scientific instruments for checking these ideas, the people dismissed them and returned to the evidence of their senses and the fairy tales of their imagination. Astronomy gave way once more to astrology. Again the scholars pictured the earth as the motionless center of the universe, and the moon and the sun and the planets as rotating chandeliers around an earthly throne. Over and above all these celestial chandeliers, declared the scholars of the past few centuries, lay the dome of our Celestial Palace—the vaulted ceiling of the heavens studded with the distant stars."

"You imply," the bishop said, "that this entire spectacle was invented for the benefit of our inflated human pride."

"Quite so," replied Copernicus, "and the idea had its merits as well as its defects. It allowed the meanest beggar to feel that he was a king enthroned in the center of the universe. But let me go on. Now and then an astronomer, like Aristarchus of Samos, re-echoed the idea of Pythagoras and Philolaus that the earth is a sphere

85

which moves around the sun. But very few astronomers paid any attention. Most of them preferred to live in the fairy-tale palace of their earth-centered theory."

"You realize, of course," his uncle pointed out, "that you are trying to push back an overwhelming tide of traditional thought—or, if you will, traditional prejudice. Don't forget that the greatest of the ancient astronomers, Ptolemy, held firmly to the geocentric picture of the universe."

"Yes, Ptolemy adhered to this theory, and let us humbly acknowledge the great debt we owe him. It was this man who, almost fifteen centuries ago, was able to predict the positions of the stars almost as accurately as we do them today. He was wrong, I believe, in his main theory; but such were the powers of his observation that he could read the sky almost like a book. Much of my observation, I must confess, has been lighted by the lamp of his genius."

Following this conversation, the bishop read his nephew's pamphlet, then offered him a bit of advice: "Your idea sounds very reasonable, but if I were you, Nicolas, I would withhold it from publication just now. Spend more time on the subject and do additional research on it before you venture to revolutionize human thought. The world has already waited fifteen centuries for your ideas. Let it wait a few more years."

Taking his uncle's advice, Copernicus made no effort to have his pamphlet published. He gave a few written copies to his intimate friends, who were unaware of the fact that Copernicus had just revealed to them the first dawning glory of a new scientific day. They casually glanced at the pamphlet and put it aside. It was not until the end of the nineteenth century that *The Little Commentary* was first printed from one of the two copies that fortunately survived.

Copernicus wrote another manuscript during his years at Heilsberg—a Latin translation of a number of Greek poems. The book, which he dedicated to his uncle, was printed in 1509 and was one of the first books of Greek literature that appeared in that part of Europe.

Copernicus refused to confine his interests to the monastery cloister. He thoroughly enjoyed his role as a courtier at his uncle's castle, which was situated on a cliff overlooking the Alle River. A forest surrounding the castle was filled with all sorts of wild game—a boon to most of the courtiers except Copernicus. He took no joy in killing for sport. However, he did find pleasure in walks around a lake in front of the castle, admiring the oaks and the beeches reflected in the tranquil waters.

He especially enjoyed the companionship of his uncle's numerous retainers, whom he usually met in the great dining hall. At the court of Bishop Watzelrode, din-

ing was a formal ceremony, but it was not dull. When the
bell rang at noontime, everybody waited for the bishop
to emerge from his apartment. The first hint that he was
ready came from the dogs who were unleashed from
their kennels. Their barking was a signal for the courtiers
to stop their conversation. The doors were swung open
and the bishop appeared looking pompous in his ecclesiastical stole and miter. The courtiers, lined up behind
him, solemnly escorted him to the hall.

As soon as he arrived, his servants offered him a golden
washbasin and a towel. After washing his hands and of-
fering a public prayer, the bishop sat down on an ele-
vated chair.

The dignitaries and lesser courtiers then ranged themselves, in the order of their importance, around the nine
tables in the dining hall. At the first table sat the bishop,
together with the chief justice of Ermland, Copernicus,
the abbots, knights and chaplains, the general of the
army, and the bishop's guests of honor.

The next four tables were reserved for the less honored
guests and the lower officials of the castle, including the
chief forester and the chief fisherman of Ermland, as well
as the head cooks and the tutors of the courtiers' children.

And then came three tables for the servants—the
coachmen, stable hands, waiters, carvers and the motley

throng of attendants within the castle and caretakers of the castle grounds. At the last of the servants' tables there was always a group of poor men whom the bishop had selected as the recipients of his bounty for the day.

And, finally, came the ninth table reserved for the entertainers of the castle—singers, dancers, gypsies, actors, bear-tamers, jugglers, tight-rope walkers, magicians and clowns. These entertainers served as the light dessert to the heavy food, and Copernicus, as his uncle's doctor, heartily approved the idea.

The bishop remained morose and, in spite of his nephew's ministrations, his health kept declining steadily. Copernicus suggested a change of scenery for a while. "It will do you good, Uncle Lucas, to get away from your duties for a period of relaxation and fun."

At first the bishop refused to listen to such advice. "My work is too important to my flock. Who will care for them while I am away?"

At the persistence of Copernicus, however, the bishop finally consented. An opportunity had presented itself to get him away from Heilsberg: the marriage of King Sigismund and the coronation of the young queen. Both the bishop and his nephew were invited to the double ceremony. "I am not quite certain whether I ought to go," said Lucas Watzelrode. "The king and I, you know, are not on the best of terms."

"But this is precisely the reason why you *should* go," argued Copernicus. "It will give both of you an opportunity for a better understanding."

"I don't know," the bishop still hesitated. "I wouldn't feel quite at ease in the king's presence. We'd look at each other like a couple of cocks preparing for a fight. But you, Nicolas, ought to go by all means. The king likes you. He will be in a festive mood, and your presence on such an occasion may help to predispose him a little in my own favor."

"I refuse to go without you, and that's final! Do you realize how insulted he will be if we refuse his invitation? An invitation from the king, you know, is a royal command."

The bishop finally agreed to go to the wedding, accompanied by Copernicus. It was in the winter of 1512 that the two arrived at the royal palace in Kraków. By comparison, Heilsberg Castle was a mere flicker of a candle against the blazing sun. The glory of the king was in keeping with the splendor of the palace. At that time Poland was regarded as the mightiest nation of Eastern Europe and its ruler was hailed as Sigismund the Great. Four years before his marriage he had won a brilliant victory over the Russians, and one of the principal features at the wedding ceremony was a pageant in honor of that event.

The pageant started at noon, immediately following the wedding ceremony, and lasted for two hours. After it was over, the guests sat down to dinner, a long-drawn-out banquet starting with Hungarian soup, which was served at two, and continuing through twenty-seven courses down to preserved fruits and marzipan, which ended the festival at midnight.

Copernicus, sitting next to his uncle, began to be worried about the bishop's health, for it was obvious that the rich food and the excitement were too much for him. After the banquet Lucas Watzelrode begged to be excused from further festivities, which were scheduled to last till dawn. The next morning the bishop insisted upon returning to Heilsberg at once. "I shall not be able to attend the coronation of the queen," he told Nicolas, "but I want you to remain as my representative. You can explain that I had to leave because of poor health."

"How can I let you go without me?" asked Nicolas. "You may need medical care on the trip home."

"Nonsense! When you get back to Heilsberg, you'll find me stronger than ever. You know our Polish proverb: 'When the doctor's at rest, the patient feels best.'"

Copernicus did not want to alarm his uncle by insisting that he accompany him, so he remained for the cor-

91

onation while his uncle started with his retinue for Heilsberg.

On the return trip the bishop stopped at Torún, planning to visit some of his old friends in his native city. Shortly after his arrival he suffered a severe heart attack and three days later he was dead.

Copernicus was hastily summoned from Kraków when the bishop's illness took a turn for the worse, but he arrived too late. Those who had attended the bishop at the end told Copernicus that he had expressed his concern about one thing in particular: "I had hoped to live long enough to appoint Nicolas Bishop in my place."

"Apparently," said Nicolas, "it is God's will that I remain an obscure canon for life." And then he added quietly, "To tell the truth, it is my own will too."

Chapter 8

A FEW WEEKS after his uncle's death, his mother died and Copernicus returned to his medical and canonical duties at the Frauenburg Cathedral. Like the bishop's castle at Heilsberg, it had also been the target of repeated assaults by the Knights of the Teutonic Order. Finally the cathedral had been fortified with a massive wall and a number of towers, which served as lookouts against the invasions of the enemy.

Copernicus chose one of those towers as his living quarters as well as his astronomical observation post, and his brother lived in another one. Before long, however, Andreas was stricken with leprosy—the disease he had so dreaded when he was a student at Bologna. For a time Nicolas tried his medical skill on his brother, but in vain. The other canons, panicked by the fear of contamination, clamored for his departure from their chapter. Andreas received an official leave of absence from the cathedral—which actually meant an unofficial expulsion from society. At that time there were no hospitals for anyone afflicted with that dreaded disease. Andreas became an aimless wanderer over the face of the earth.

Copernicus wanted to accompany his brother on his solitary pilgrimage, but Andreas would not permit it. "My own career is over, Nicolas. There is no sense in sacrificing yours along with mine. You have important work to do."

"The world can spare my work."

"You are wrong, my brother. My talents are limited—I am but one among millions of other ordinary creatures. We come and go like bubbles on the surface of a stream; and when we disappear, the course of the stream remains still unchanged. But you are different. Your own life may influence the lives of all the generations to come. I want you to stay here and continue your studies. My last days

94

will be happier at the thought that you are going ahead with your work."

Nicolas recognized the wisdom of these words, yet he was heartbroken at the thought that his brother was embarking upon his last lonely journey. They had always been close to each other. Andreas, however, made an effort to ease the pain of their final separation. "Do you know, Nicolas," he said, "I feel that I am a part of you. Whatever triumphs you achieve, I will be able to share with you. Many years after both of us are gone, perhaps the memory of your name will cast a reflected glow upon my own."

Copernicus watched through a film of tears as his brother started slowly toward the carriage. Before he took his seat, however, Andreas turned around. "Do you remember the time in Bologna when both of us heard a leper's bell? It was I, not you, who shrank away in terror. But, Nicolas," Andreas added with a slight smile, "I am no longer afraid. Strange, isn't it, how we tremble at danger when it threatens us from a distance, and find the courage to face it when it actually arrives?"

Nicolas smiled back in answer to his brother's courageous words. "Go with the peace of God," he said, holding up his right hand in a gesture of benediction. He watched the carriage disappear in the mist. Andreas' departure was leaving a painful void in his heart. First his uncle, then his mother and now his brother. Copernicus felt alone in the world.

He went back to his tower and sat down to write the preface of his projected book. It would be many years, perhaps, before he could begin the book itself, and most likely he would have to revise the preface again and again. But the words he wrote on that day would serve as a guide to his future study. He would follow this guide as he went along, charting his course and correcting his errors whenever he found it necessary to change his direction. "I shall explore the rapid course of the moon, the earth's brother," he wrote, "and the whole sky and the planets—the wonderful creation of the Father of all. Starting from a single principle, I shall explore the hidden causes of things . . ."

Behind the great mystery was the creation of the Father of all. "It is His eternal love that guides the pathways of the stars and the footsteps of His children."

Copernicus fell upon his knees as the tears streamed down from his eyes. "Our Father in Heaven," he prayed, "keep a loving watch over Andreas, and let him not stray beyond the touch of Thy gentle hand."

After his brother's departure Nicolas became more than ever absorbed in his studies and his duties at the cathedral, his anguish temporarily forgotten in the excitement that followed the election and the inauguration of the new bishop. For a while there had been a slender chance that Copernicus might get the post. But he was no politician and, with his uncle gone, there was no powerful voice to plead in his behalf. His candidacy was passed over, and a more ambitious man secured the post.

Copernicus was relieved that destiny had bypassed him. An order from the new bishop, however, added to his duties if not to his distinctions; he was made canon of two additional parishes—Allenstein and Mehlsack—as well as of Frauenburg. His work was thus trebled, and his leisure for study drastically reduced. It was his daily routine to ride out with his assistants over the three parishes, to settle the quarrels among the farmers, to listen to their grievances and to make the necessary adjustments in the transfer of property from hand to hand.

In addition to these duties, for which he was well paid, he dispensed his medical services throughout the district, usually without charge. Again and again, when he returned from his circuit at night, he was so spent that he could hardly stand on his feet. Yet, even then, there was no rest for him. Waiting for him were patients from the local parish. "What can I do?" he said to his housekeeper, who cautioned him not to work so hard. "They come to me at all hours of the day and night. I have not the heart to turn them away."

In view of all this, it was a miracle that he found the

97

strength for his astronomical observations. Night after night, when the world around him was at rest, he climbed to the top of his tower at the Frauenburg Cathedral. The spot was well situated, since it opened upon a vast half-circle of sky over a wide expanse of the sea. Frequently, however, the thick northern mists of the Baltic obstructed his view. At such times he longed for the clear skies of Italy. Yet throughout the years, in spite of his handicaps, he continued to piece together his new picture of the heavens. His observations and calculations only served to convince him that the earth must have two motions—a daily rotation on its axis and a yearly revolution around the sun. These two motions helped to explain most of the positions of the stars and the planets at various times, but not all of them. For Copernicus made one important mistake in his calculations. He believed that each of the planets, including the earth, moved in a circular orbit instead of an ellipse. Thus he was unable to account for the apparent discrepancies between the motion of the earth and the motion of some of the other planets, such as Mars. He had observed, as had Ptolemy, that at times that planet seemed to stand still or to move backward in its relation to the earth. The simple explanation, of course, is that Mars takes about two years to revolve around the sun, while the earth moves twice as fast in an orbit that is half as large as Mars'. Therefore, when the earth overtakes Mars, the latter seems to stand still and then to move backward. It remained for Johannes Kepler (1571-1630) to demonstrate the elliptical paths of the planets and to correct the Copernican theory.

Troubled by his miscalculations, Copernicus persisted in his efforts to find the flaw in his theory. He continued to believe, however, that he had come closer to the truth than any astronomer before him. He drew a chart of the universe, with the sun in the center surrounded by six circles of planets and stars. This was a tremendous simplification of the ten thousand circles which Ptolemy had required to explain the clockwork of the heavens.

As his heliocentric theory of the universe gradually became public knowledge, Copernicus found himself the center of a battle between the truths of astronomy and the pretensions of astrology. People lived under the sway of the astrologers, who insisted that the wheel of a man's fortune depended upon the rotating circles of the sun and the stars. They kept the world in a continual tremor with their predictions of wars, earthquakes, floods and other disasters, most of which never came to pass. Even when people witnessed the failure of astrology, they continued to believe in it. A famous scientist of the day, Jerome Cardano, wrote his autobiography at the age of seventy-six. In this book he stated that his entire youth had been ruined because an astrologer had predicted his

99

death before his fortieth year. Yet, amazingly enough, Cardano consulted an astrologer about the "most propitious date" for the printing of his autobiography.

Carlo Poggia, Copernicus' friend from Bologna, had become a professor of astronomy, but supplemented his income as an astrologer. Many students of science concealed their true knowledge under the mask of pseudo-science, insisting that it was the only way they could make a comfortable living. That was the practical ground upon which Poggia tried to defend himself when Copernicus upbraided him for his surrender to superstition.

"Nobody respects me for explaining the past and the present," he said, "but everybody admires me for predicting the future."

He then related a hoax he had perpetrated upon the public. "I told the people that I had witnessed in the clouds a spectacle that portended an imminent plague or war or some other great calamity. I vividly described my vision—four thousand galloping dogs that symbolized the soldiers of an invading enemy; a multitude of headless men, women and children that represented our own people slain by the foe; and a monster of the sea, with the head and horns of a devil, the tail of a fish, and the arms of a satyr who dragged young girls away from their homes into strange lands."

"Did you actually see this?" asked Copernicus with a skeptical smile.

"Who knows? The formations of the clouds are so fantastic, and the figures keep changing so rapidly, that anybody with a vivid imagination can see almost anything in those momentary paintings in the air."

"And of course," said Copernicus scornfully, "the people did not question your vision."

"How could they? Since there was nobody present at the time of the vision to disprove it, the people had to take my word for it."

"But how could people *believe* a prophecy based upon your vision?"

"I'm surprised that a wise man like you can be so naïve. Remember the Latin adage—'*Populus vult decipi*' —The public wants to be deceived. Most of the prophecies of the astrologers are merely shrewd guesses as to what is likely to happen. Take my own case. I am well aware of the occurrence of wars and plagues and all sorts of other calamities, so I was pretty safe in my prediction. The only thing I did was to base a natural fact upon a supernatural fiction. The public swallowed the hoax and loved it; so did many of the scholars. I got a promotion at the university as a result of my profound wisdom."

Copernicus sadly admitted the unscientific status of science in his day—a slender structure of truth supported by a shifting foundation of falsehood. The clouds were expected to foreshadow history, the dead were conjured up to advise the living, and the stars were studied to account for the affairs of men. No wonder the Italian historian, Guicciardini, wrote: "The astrologers are praised if they tell one truth among a hundred lies, while the scientists are blamed if they tell one lie among a hundred truths."

In the midst of his work at Frauenburg, Copernicus received word that his brother, Andreas, had died. In an effort to ease his sorrow, Copernicus buried himself more than ever in his studies. But he clearly recalled Andreas' words the day he had departed: "Do you know, Nicolas, I feel that I am a part of you." There was a deep truth in those words. But just as he was a part of his brother, Andreas was a part of him, and with his brother's death, something died within him. He was never the same again. Although his scientific mind rebelled against a problem to which he could find no answer, he knew that he would never be able to solve the great mystery of death.

Chapter 9

COPERNICUS LIVED AT Frauenburg for the rest of his life. He called the little town "the remotest corner of the earth," yet he did not have need for extended physical travel in order to reach out toward the widest horizons of human thought. "The most fascinating journeys are those of the mind," he told himself as he sat upon an open-air platform outside his tower for his nightly adventures among the stars. To understand the whole universe, he felt, one must have a universal mind. One must see the world as a united whole and not as a conglomeration of divided parts. He added another paragraph to his preface:

> The Scientist who would examine the various phenomena individually, without regard to the order and close dependency among them, might be compared to an artist who would borrow fragments, such as hands, feet and other parts of the body which, though truly painted by a master's hand, represented different bodies: and these incongruous fragments, when put together, would rather fit the picture of a monster than that of a man.

Copernicus believed that a new understanding of the universe as a harmonious, patterned structure was even more important than a new system of astronomy. Many years later, in 1896, the great astronomer Simon Newcomb wrote: "The real significance of the Copernican system lies in the greatness of this conception [of a patterned universe] rather than in the fact of the [astronomical] discovery itself."

It was the aim of Copernicus' life to establish the world as a place of harmony, friendliness, peace. He wanted the nations of the earth, like the stars in the heavens, to move in their appointed courses without clashing with one another. The little state in which he lived, Ermland, was caught between the ambitions of the Polish king and the Teutonic Grand Master. In 1519, shortly after the death of Andreas, the friction between the two rulers came to a head. After capturing the Ermland town of Braunsberg, the Teutonic Knights threatened to overrun the entire state and invade Poland itself. King Sigismund suggested a truce and appointed the Bishop of Frauenburg to mediate between himself and the Grand Master.

Too ill at the time to attend the conference, the bishop asked Copernicus, who was used to diplomatic missions of this sort, to take his place. Copernicus had often undertaken to settle the differences between his uncle and the king. But this conference presented a more serious problem—a vital question of peace or war.

The Grand Master received the visitor from Frauenburg with a sarcastic smile. He was a small man with frowning black eyes, thin lips and a whining voice that made him sound like an ill-behaved child. His gestures, too, were like those of a child who insisted on having his way. People usually agreed with him because they were afraid of his hysterical outbursts if they dissented.

Thus he strutted about like a cockerel in a farmyard while everybody drew back in terror. Intoxicated as he was with his recent conquests, he felt that he would have no difficulty in bringing the unpretentious, soft-spoken cleric to his knees. He was quite accustomed to dealing with people who believed in turning the other cheek. A little flattery, a little subtlety and a great deal of bluster —these, he thought, would be all the arguments he needed to keep Copernicus in his place.

He started with flattery by presenting a formal letter to "the worthy, most learned Sir Nicolas Copernicus" in which he promised him "our free, safe and Christian conduct within our Order's land." But when Copernicus arrived at Braunsberg, he politely thanked the Grand Master for his words and then sharply rebuked him for his deeds. "This scene of our conference," he reminded the Grand Master, "is not the land of your Order. It is the property of our Church."

"It is ours by virtue of conquest," insisted the Grand Master.

"There is never any virtue in conquest, sire. Remember the words of our Lord: 'They that take the sword shall perish by the sword.'"

"I don't subscribe to these words! The rulers of the world are not the meek but the mighty. The Teutonic Order is destined to rule—not only within our own generation but for a thousand years!"

"A thousand years, sire, are but as a day in the eyes of the Lord. But I see you have no faith in the Bible. Let me, therefore, call your attention to the facts of history.

Aggression does not pay. All the aggressive nations of the past have come to an early death. And the reason for this is very simple. Hatred begets hatred; bloodshed provokes bloodshed. The conqueror arouses a spirit of revenge within the hearts of the conquered. This vengeful spirit festers and grows and infuriates the victims of the aggressor until finally they fall upon him in their wrath. Thus the victor of yesterday becomes the victim of today."

"You cite history, Herr Copernicus, but you name no names. Can you prove your assertion that the glory of conquest leads only to disaster and disgrace?"

"Yes, indeed, sire. History has proved my assertion again and again. Busy as you are with your dreams, perhaps you have not had the time to ascertain the facts. But let me recall for you just a few instances that prove a universal truth. Assyria, Egypt, Persia, Sparta, Macedonia, Carthage, Rome—all these nations committed national suicide through their aggressiveness. They flourished for a time and then were submerged in a whirlpool of blood. Their conquering weapon, you see, was a double-edged sword. It cut down not only the victim but the victor as well."

The Grand Master looked upon Copernicus with a mingled feeling of admiration and contempt. This Polish canon, he had to admit, had a keen mind and a glib tongue. But, after all, might was might and the soldiers ruled the world. Perhaps Copernicus was correct in his outlook on history, but he was impractical, a stargazer.

"When the fruits of today are sweet to the taste," he said, "why bother about the pains they may bring tomorrow?"

Today the Teutonic Knights held the upper hand. Ermland was almost in their grasp, and perhaps all Poland if the Grand Master maintained a firm grip. How dare this rebellious little preacher talk to him as an equal? Nay, as a superior!

"Do you know," he threatened, "that you are entirely in my power? A single word from me, and you are a dead man!"

"As to this, sire, you are quite correct. I could die at your command. But my truth would live on."

The Grand Master's eyes shot fire, yet he refrained from further threats. He had given Copernicus a letter of safe-conduct and, with all his insolence as a conqueror, he still retained something of his gallantry as a knight. "I didn't quite mean what I said, Herr Copernicus. I shall respect your person as the ambassador of your Church. Will you therefore state briefly what message you carry."

"We request that you withdraw from our Church property."

108

"Denied. Whatever we have conquered we are determined to hold."

"We also request," said Copernicus quietly, "that you refrain from further attacks on our Church territory."

"Again denied," was the blunt reply. "We are on the march and nothing shall stop us!"

"Then there is nothing more to be said," observed Copernicus.

"Yes, there is. Tell your bishop that we demand from him and from the entire chapter of canons an oath of allegiance to the Teutonic Knights and especially to me, their Grand Master."

"This, sire, you will never get from us. We owe but a single supreme allegiance—to God."

And so Copernicus returned to Frauenburg, and the Grand Master proceeded with his plans to overrun Ermland. With that state in his possession, Poland would be his next goal.

He ordered his army to march from Frauenburg to Allenstein—one of the three districts over which Copernicus had been appointed canonical overseer. Though a passionate lover of peace, Copernicus was determined to resist the Teutonic Knights. He asked the other canons to help organize the defense of the castle, but they had no stomach for the fight. Most of them fled to places of safety. It remained for Copernicus to prepare the defense, command the troops that had been hastily recruited from the surrounding territory, and lead them if necessary into battle against the Knights.

Meanwhile the invaders had been sweeping across Ermland, devastating farms and killing peasants. Here and there a handful of heroic defenders checked the advancing horde—but only for a short time.

It seemed a hopeless fight for Copernicus and his little band. One of his colleagues who had fled from Ermland managed to forward to Allenstein a few crude guns and a small supply of powder and shot. Around one of the guns was wrapped a pathetic note: *Don't surrender the castle!* Copernicus smiled grimly as he read those words. It was like the encouragement of a spectator who sat safely above the arena and shouted to the victims below not to surrender to the lions.

Yet Copernicus succeeded in his defense. After an unsuccessful siege of several. months the Grand Master withdrew his troops. The dreaded name of the war lord who had threatened to extend his rule for a thousand years became a laughingstock. An unprofessional soldier, a man devoted to peace, had pricked the bubble of his military pretensions. He signed a truce that was to last for several years and during this cooling-off period he had a chance for sober reflection. He never attacked Copernicus again.

Even under siege, the astronomer was able now and then to snatch a few hours for his observation of the stars, and it was during that time that he penned the following thoughts on the universe:

The motions of the heavenly bodies are natural and not violent. Whatever is in accordance with nature, therefore, is nonviolent. Things upon which violence or an external force is exerted must become annihilated and cannot long exist. But whatever happens without violence remains in good condition and moves in concert with the general harmony of the world.

The entire universe "forms a unity and a whole," the underlying purpose of which is not destructive upheaval but constructive order. His scientific speculation as well as his religious conviction led Copernicus to a single formula: "The basic pattern of the universe is not war, but peace."

111

Chapter 10

DEDICATED AS HE was to two of the most unworldly professions—astronomy and religion—Copernicus was nonetheless a man of the world, with interest in the material as well as in the spiritual problems of mankind. When the invasion of Ermland had been repulsed, he superintended the rebuilding of the ruined estates and the resettling of the peasants on their farms. As "Commissioner for Ermland," by appointment of the bishop, his job was to hearten the souls of the people, bind their wounds, restore their health and draw up an account of the property damage inflicted by the Knights. The Grand Master, his pride considerably deflated by his defeat, had promised to make restitution for his unprovoked attacks.

Copernicus had an able assistant in his task of restoration: his fellow canon, Tiedemann Giese. This man, thirteen years older than Copernicus, was one of the few supporters of Copernicus' revolutionary theory of the universe. He encouraged him in his astronomical studies and volunteered to relieve him of some of his official burdens.

At that period, when a great religious controversy was raging all over Europe, Copernicus and Giese were both tolerant toward the adherents of other faiths. An intrepid young priest, Martin Luther, had broken away from the Catholic Church to establish an organization of his own—the Protestant Church, or the Church of the Protesters. For a time Catholics and Protestants confined their controversy to a heated debate, without any bloodshed. But as the argument became more violent, the less temperate partisans began to quarrel and then to fight. Before long the controversy had developed into a series of savage wars. Many people foolishly believed that the only way to convince their opponents of the truth was to kill them. On both sides, however, a number of enlightened souls refused to be drawn into the quarrel. Among them were Copernicus and Tiedemann Giese, as well as their superior, the Bishop of Ermland. In the midst of the turmoil it was difficult, even dangerous, for the three men to openly discuss the controversy. Yet they frequently talked about it among themselves.

"Luther is a learned man," the bishop pointed out. "We may disagree with his ideas and we have a right to tell him so. But he has an equal right to disagree with ours."

"If he has done evil," observed Giese, "God will call him to account. It is not for us to usurp His divine judgment."

"What I can't grasp," said the gentle Copernicus, "is our human stupidity in our effort to understand the divine. We are all trying to reach heaven in different ways —but certainly the way of bloodshed is not one of them. How can we resort to war in our endeavor to serve the Prince of Peace?"

Yet the wave of bloodshed—both sides invoking the help of God—continued to sweep across Europe. The more fanatical among Luther's followers threatened to "cleanse the world" of its monks and priests, while the less moderate among the adherents of the Pope vowed "to uproot the heretics" of the new sect.

"The wild animals of the forest," Giese said sadly, "behave more gently to their kind than do many Christians to theirs."

Before long the religious war turned into a political conflict. Peasants rebelled against princes, serfs against masters, the poor against the rich. "Go to it!" cried Thomas Münzer, one of the more fanatical leaders of the Reformation. "Go to it! Beloved brothers, do not be moved by pity! Let not your sword become cold for lack of steaming blood! Strike your blows upon the tyrants, hurl down their power!"

The German peasants, roused to fury by such hysterical speeches, turned with equal fury upon the Catholic and the Protestant churches, and in their blindness burned down their own hovels as well as the palaces of the kings.

After a stormy career of preaching a radical doctrine, Münzer was defeated and brought to trial. When the judge reminded him of the numerous victims tortured and killed at his command, he replied with a vicious laugh: "They got what they wanted!"

"Very well," retorted the judge, "you will get what *you* want." And he sentenced Münzer to be beheaded.

The Peasants' War did not win them the liberties they sought. Their uprising failed, and over a hundred thousand of them were slaughtered, all in the name of liberty and the Lord. "May God forgive us," prayed Copernicus, "for taking His name in vain!"

During the Reformation, Copernicus kept steadily at his development of a new theory of the universe. However violently the various factions disagreed on other matters, they were united in their opposition to his notion that the earth moved and the sun stood still. Martin Luther, who was battling for his new ideas on religion, clung to the Ptolemaic theory of astronomy and denounced Copernicus as "the new scientist who wants to prove that the earth goes round, and not the sun; just as if someone sitting in a moving wagon or ship were to suppose that he was at rest, and the Earth and the trees were moving past him . . . this fool is trying to turn the whole science of astronomy upside down. But it was the sun and not the earth which Joshua commanded to stand still."

Nor did Copernicus find support within his own religious order. Bishop Fabian von Lossainen was liberal in his religious ideas but conservative in his scientific beliefs. He argued that the new ideas were contrary to the teaching of the Old Testament, and warned Copernicus against "brazenly overthrowing an established fact with an unproved conjecture." When Bishop Fabian died in 1523, his successor, Mauritius Ferber, was even more hostile toward the ideas of Copernicus. He made every effort to stifle what he called "the canon's heretical thoughts."

Even among scholars the Copernican theory was almost universally condemned. The leader in the opposition camp was Philip Melanchthon, a German Humanist who was at the time a professor of Greek at the University of Wittenberg. "The babblings of the Polish astronomer," declared Melanchthon, "are contrary to the plan of God and the logic of mankind. Our eyes bear witness against Copernicus, and the thousand-year consensus of learned scholars proves that his theory is absurd." Several of the contemporary writers prepared lampoons and plays in which they depicted Copernicus as a clown dancing around the sun "which, in his stupidity, he regards as standing still."

Such was the general atmosphere of turbulence, revolution, hostility and ridicule in which Copernicus lived and worked. In the entire world there were only two men who dared to favor his ideas openly. They were the Protestant Rheticus and the Catholic Giese.

Rheticus, like Melanchthon, taught at the Lutheran University of Wittenberg. This young German scholar, whose name was Georg Joachim, called himself Rheticus after his birthplace in Rhaetia, a province in the Tyrolese Mountains of Austria. A scientist of extraordinary talent, he had been appointed a professor of mathematics at the university at the age of twenty-two.

Though Wittenberg was one of the strongholds of the Protestant Reformation, Rheticus was more interested in scientific investigation than in religious controversy. He was tolerant toward people of all faiths and, unlike many of his colleagues, was willing to examine all sorts of ideas, from all kinds of people, with equal impartiality.

When Rheticus heard of Copernicus' investigations, he began to correspond with him. After three years he asked the university for a leave of absence in order to visit "the lonely man at Frauenburg who was walking among the stars." As a result of this visit Rheticus became an ardent champion of the Copernican theory.

Copernicus' second champion, Tiedemann Giese, tried to bridge the gap not only between the old thinkers and the new but between the old religion and the new. His main ambition in life was to reconcile rather than to inflame conflicting views. He implored scholars and churchmen alike to look upon one another's ideas with respect. He wrote a pamphlet in which he made a strong plea for mutual tolerance. At first he circulated the pamphlet only in manuscript, but at the insistence of Copernicus he finally published it. He sent printed copies of the work to friends and adversaries alike. In the preface he wrote: "I entirely reject the battle between the various religious camps." And then, in the spirit of a true believer, he gently chided both sides:

118

When everything proceeds in wild turmoil and rebellion, who is there left to build? What do we find but general confusion as a result of all this quarreling and defamation? While referring constantly to the spirit of God, we are estranging ourselves entirely from the spirit of love. Love endureth all things—it is not eager to inflict harm. If only the Protestants were filled with this Christian spirit toward the Catholics, and the Catholics toward the Protestants, this tragedy of hatred and bloodshed could so easily be averted . . . How good it will be if the two Churches can live together in peace just like the two Sisters, Faith and Love. Then we shall speak as with one voice—the voice of God!

These words fell upon deaf ears. The tolerance of Giese and Rheticus and the wisdom of Copernicus were out of tune with the times. The voice of reason was drowned out in the tumult. Added to the general confusion, a wave of terror began to sweep over Europe when astrologers predicted the end of the world, which was to occur on February 11, 1524. Professor Stoeffler, of Tübingen, was the first to foresee this catastrophe "in a conjunction of the planets under the sign of Pisces"— the constellation of the Fishes. This conjunction, he prophesied, would bring about a deluge more terrible than that of the Bible. This time not even a Noah's Ark would enable anyone to survive.

Almost everybody believed the professor's warning. Yet a number of people, hoping that they, like Noah, would be able to outride the flood, started building arks and stocking them with crates of food. Thousands of timid souls flocked to astrologers to seek advice. They paid exorbitant fees for such counsel—voluntarily, in most cases, since their money would mean nothing in the event of the world's destruction. The astrologers were not reluctant to accept the fees, in case their predictions might prove to be wrong. One of them bought a vineyard with the money he earned for his dire predictions. It was situated on a mountaintop, again in case . . . The astrologers apparently were more practical than profound.

Almost alone among the unbelievers in Professor Stoeffler's prophecy was Copernicus. One of his colleagues at the cathedral reminded him that the world was coming to an end and advised him to spend his time praying instead of studying the stars. But Copernicus merely smiled and said, "Let it end."

His calmness was due to the conviction that the astrologers were wrong. They retaliated with an avalanche of vituperation against the "radical disbeliever in the established system of the stars."

The "day of doom"—February 11—arrived on the wings of a storm. Thousands of people huddled in the churches awaiting the end. Many of them, in their illogical terror, felt that Copernicus was somehow responsible for their trouble. "It is men like him who arouse the anger of the Lord!" exclaimed one of their superstitious leaders. "Copernicus has tried to upset the order of the world, and God will punish all of us for his sins!"

As the hours of the dreaded day passed by, the fury of the storm increased—and the terror of the populace increased along with it. But Copernicus spent the day writing a pamphlet to defend his mathematical calculations about the revolutions of the planets. "Astronomy, the queen of the sciences, is based upon almost all the branches of mathematics," and the verdict of these different branches is always the same: The old theories of astronomy have failed to explain the length of the month and the year. "As a result," Copernicus went on, "we are uncertain about the exact date on which we are to celebrate our Christmas and Easter and other holidays. Our calendar, our religious observances, our agriculture, our daily mode of life—all these are dependent upon a new and true knowledge of astronomy."

It also could have revealed the foolishness of the astrologers' prediction about the end of the world. The welfare of the world was not subject to the conjunction of the stars. The storm of February 11, 1524, produced nothing more than an ordinary snowfall. Yet most people—including the majority of scholars—still clung to their stubborn belief in astrology. And they continued to deride the "amateur astronomer who, in his folly, orders the sun to stand still!"

Chapter 11

ALTHOUGH COPERNICUS was ridiculed for his theoretical ideas, many statesmen respected him for his practical skill, for example, the way in which he had restored the ruined estates of Ermland. They began to call upon him for various kinds of advice.

One of the problems that concerned everybody at that period was the inaccuracy of the calendar. As early as the thirteenth century the great scientist Roger Bacon had declared that, if the calendar remained unchanged, people would soon feast on fast days and fast on feast days. Moreover, he continued, the dates would finally get so out of hand that Christmas would be celebrated on Easter.

The calendar in use at the time of Roger Bacon, and even at the time of Copernicus, was based upon the Julian year—named after Julius Caesar. This calendar, adopted about sixty years before the birth of Christ, was almost, but not quite, correct. The margin of error was small enough in a single year; but in the course of a century it amounted to a considerable discrepancy in the computation of time.

In the sixteenth century the leaders of Church and State had become alarmed over the inaccuracy and confusion of the calendar. Accordingly Pope Leo X called a general council of princes, professors and private individuals to straighten out this troublesome matter.

One of the men invited to this council was Copernicus, but he refused to attend. The reason he gave for his refusal was that the calendar could not be corrected until the motions of the heavenly bodies had been thoroughly and scientifically ascertained. "Since I have not as yet completed my studies on this subject," he explained, "I cannot conscientiously suggest any changes in the calendar. I shall be glad, however, to offer my opinion later on when my work is finished and I can base my suggestions upon scientific facts."

The matter was dropped at the time. Thirty-nine years after the death of Copernicus, however, Pope Gregory XIII carried out a reform of the calendar based largely upon the findings of Copernicus. In order to make the necessary adjustments in the calendar, he ordered ten days dropped out of the year 1582. And thus "everybody went to bed on October 4 of that year and got up on October 15."

Equally important with the question of the calendar in the sixteenth century was the problem of economics. A succession of wars had impoverished the masses. Inflation was riding high all over Europe. As someone has well defined it, "Inflation means merely this—whatever comes in fast goes out even faster." Business was brisk and money plentiful. Yet, due to the excessive cost of living, many people were starving.

In his work as the administrator of his parishes, Copernicus had witnessed the sufferings of the peasants. He felt that the root of the evil was the misuse of money. The world did not understand the simple principles of economics. As a young man he had been interested in the commercial problems of his brother-in-law at Kraków. His practical turn of mind had enabled him to solve those problems and provide his brother-in-law with a sound financial basis for business. He frequently discussed, with Giese and some of the other canons, the economical machinery that regulated their country.

"How did it happen," asked Giese, "that a scientist like yourself became interested in financial problems?"

"It's quite simple. I am concerned with the pattern of the world, which includes the harmonious movement of the stars, the health of the human body and the healthy circulation of money in the business of life."

"Do you mean to tell us," asked another canon, Sculteti, "that there can be an *unhealthy* circulation of money?"

"Yes, indeed. There are times when money, like the human body, is subject to disease. At such times it is our business to cure it."

"I am afraid," smiled Giese, "that you are allowing your role as a physician to run away with you in other fields. Surely you don't mean that there is a science of money, just as there is a science of medicine?"

"That is precisely what I do mean. I admit that this idea is unfamiliar to many, but someday the world will realize that there are definite laws that govern all motion—whether it is the change of position between the stars or the exchange of money between man and man."

"An interesting theory," said Giese, "if you can prove it."

"I shall try to do so in a pamphlet that I am writing at this time."

Sculteti looked at Copernicus with admiration. "You are the most amazing man I have ever met! Religious officer, civil administrator, astronomer, soldier, philosopher, physician and now economist!"

Copernicus shrugged his shoulders. "Life is short, you know, and I am merely trying to reach out in as many directions as possible. I know only too well how little I can travel in any of these directions."

He finished his pamphlet on economics and demonstrated a simple fact that should have been obvious to keen financial minds. He stated that when the value of money falls, goods become twice as expensive. Workers cannot afford to buy the goods and therefore demand higher wages. The higher wages result in still higher prices for the goods. And thus there arises a vicious spiral of inflation: higher wages, higher prices, less value to the currency, and the cycle starts again.

The Polish and Prussian governments, intrigued by the ideas of Copernicus, invited him to an economic conference arranged for the purpose of stemming the rising tide of inflation.

Copernicus accepted the invitation and asked Tiedemann Giese and Sculteti to accompany him. On the journey he explained to them what, in his opinion, was the particular disease that had undermined the financial health of Europe at that time. "Every city, like Torún and Kraków and Danzig, stubbornly insists upon the right to coin its own money."

"What we need, I suppose," suggested Giese, "is for all the cities to agree upon a single standard of coinage?"

"Precisely," nodded Copernicus. "This holds true not only for all the cities but for each country. But that isn't the whole trouble. The various cities and countries not only stick to their separate coinage, but they debase the value of their money."

"What do you mean?" asked Sculteti, still not grasping the whole subject clearly.

"Just this," Copernicus explained: "Several cities and countries, in order to increase the number of coins in circulation, have been mixing base metals with precious metals."

"Like copper and gold?"

"Yes."

When Copernicus stood up to address the members of the conference, he tried to point out two vital mistakes in the system of coining money. "In the first place, you mix base metals with precious metals. In the second place, you melt down the coins you have and then refashion the metal into a greater number of coins. You therefore think you are richer because you have more coins, but actually you are poorer because each coin has less value. You are like the stingy farmer who sows weeds among his grain in order to raise a bigger crop."

While Copernicus was speaking, several of the officials at the conference began to whisper about him.

"Who is this man?"

"A canon."

"A canon? What does he know about money?"

"He is a nephew of the late Bishop Watzelrode, who was a very rich man."

"But how does that make him an expert on coinage?"

"I really don't know."

"They say he's an amateur astronomer."

"That explains it. A stargazer!"

"The next thing we know, he'll be making coins out of stars!"

A general guffaw interrupted the meeting. The presiding officer motioned for silence, and Copernicus went on:

"Among the innumerable evils which bring about the ruin of a country, four are to be regarded as most important—inner dissension, high mortality due to sickness and war, barrenness of the soil, and deterioration of money. The first three evils are obvious to most people. But the fourth, which results from the coinage of bad

money, is noted only by a few . . . because the states
exposed to this evil do not succumb at once to its first
attack, but perish gradually and imperceptibly . . ."

Another flurry of whispers and another request from
the presiding officer to let him speak without interruption.

"In the past," continued Copernicus, "a pound of silver was coined into twenty marks. Now it is coined into
thirty or even forty marks. This results in increased living
expenses for everybody. The poor cannot buy bread, and
even the rich are harvesting a crop of chaff instead of
grain. Thus, when you allow your money to lose its
value, you believe you are cheating others—but actually
you are cheating yourselves."

"What would you have us do?" asked the presiding
officer.

"Abandon the system of separate currency in every
city, or even in every country. Call in all the debased
coins and establish new coinage with a guaranteed
amount of precious metal for each coin. Above all, appoint a single authority to issue these coins, with uniform weight and value, for the united benefit of mankind."

Here again was Copernicus' idea of *unity*—a single
standard of values for all the world, a single sense of

compassion for all the poor, a single law of motion for all the stars.

But once again his vision was far too advanced for understanding in his day. The presiding officer of the conference referred Copernicus' currency recommendation to a special committee. Here the selfish interests of the various communities had their way. Blind to the advantages of cooperation and goaded by their private greed, the leaders of the separate cities and nations continued to coin their own money and hamper the general prosperity of the world.

It was not until several years after the death of Copernicus that his monetary theory became recognized as an economic principle. Formulated by Sir Thomas Gresham and known to this day as Gresham's Law, this principle states that the minting of bad money drives out good money. It was not Gresham, however, but Copernicus who first expressed this vital principle of economics.

Chapter 12

COPERNICUS CONTINUED to work in comparative obscurity. His religious belief, like his scientific instinct, urged him in the direction of harmony—one God, one moral principle of love, one universal law that embraced heaven and earth. Whenever there was a controversy, whether in his own cathedral or in the wider world, he tried to settle it on the basis of better understanding and mutual respect. His favorite quotation from the Bible was: "Blessed are the peace-makers, for they shall be called the children of God."

132

Copernicus maintained that all people, whether Catholic or Protestant, Polish or Prussian, nobles or peasants, are the equally beloved children of God. Yet his very tolerance precipitated intolerance against him on every side. People did not want to be equal; they wanted to be superior to someone or something. Whenever he tried to reconcile two disputing parties, he displeased both. As a result, he became more and more unpopular. His opposition to religious disputes, as well as his attempt to establish new ideas about the stars, created resentment on the part of the public that kept brewing steadily until finally it broke into open derision. Spurred on by the Teutonic Knights, who still smarted under their defeat at Ermland, a schoolteacher by the name of Wilhelm Gnapheus wrote a burlesque about "the ridiculous astronomical theory of the monk at Frauenburg Cathedral."

This burlesque, entitled *Morosophus 'The Wise Fool'* was enacted in several cities of Europe. It assumed the form of a mock procession through the city streets. A throng of actors dressed as monks and beggars, led by a clown who represented Copernicus, kept shouting at the sun to stand still so that they could take a ride around it.

"But how can we ride all the way around the sun?" asks one of the beggars.

"On the little chariot of the earth," replies the impersonator of Copernicus.

"And who is to drive this chariot?"

"I, Copernicus, in my coachman's seat above the Frauenburg Cathedral."

"And how can you be sure that the houses and the trees and the mountains will follow along behind you?"

"I shall pull them with the power of my imagination."

"The power of his imagination, ha-ha!"

"But suppose you drive too fast and the earth drops away behind you?"

"Then I shall be free to fly among the stars!"

Such ridicule and mockery served at least one purpose: It aroused the curiosity of a number of people who otherwise might never have heard of Copernicus. "Who is this obscure canon of Frauenburg? And just what is the nature of his ideas?" The very attempts to discredit him served to plant the seeds of inquiry in many minds. As a consequence of the appearance of *Morosophus* in various parts of Europe, a number of requests for further information came to him from Protestant as well as from Catholic thinkers.

Among them was an Italian canon by the name of Celio Calcagnini. "I am inclined to agree with you," Calcagnini wrote to Copernicus, "that the sun, which seems to whirl and rotate, stands still and enjoys eternal rest." He did not have the courage, however, to proceed with the natural conclusion that, if the sun stands still, the earth must necessarily revolve around it.

Another scholar who became interested in Copernicus' ideas was Johann Albrecht von Widmanstetter, secretary to Pope Clement VII. This man explained the ideas of Copernicus to the Pope. Though his explanation showed that he was not opposed to those ideas, he took care not to express himself as actually supporting them.

Calcagnini and von Widmanstetter, like a few other scholars of that period, thought it was safe enough to express half-truths but dangerous to face the whole truth. Quite different, however, was the attitude of one of his more courageous disciples—Cardinal Nicolas von Schoenberg.

A Saxon who had been educated in Italy, Von Schoenberg was inspired by the teaching of Savonarola to become a Dominican monk. Through sheer ability and personal magnetism he had risen through the ranks to the position of bishop and then cardinal. After hearing about the astronomical observations of Copernicus and of the ridicule heaped upon him by the unthinking mob, he became interested to learn more about the man and his work. Copernicus was surprised to receive the following letter:

Cardinal Nicolas von Schoenberg sends his greetings to Nicolas Copernicus.

Some time ago, when I heard a number of people speaking of your amazing investigations, I conceived a regard for you. I had learned that you not only profoundly understood the teachings of the ancient astronomers, but that you had also constructed a new world system.

In this system, as I have heard, you teach that the earth is moving, that the sun occupies the center of the world, and that the moon revolves about the sun in an annual orbit.

These conceptions of yours fill me with the greatest admiration. Therefore may I earnestly beg you, highly learned man, to communicate your discoveries to those desirous of knowledge, and to send me, as soon as possible, the result of your mighty meditations upon the universe.

If you do me this favor, you will learn that I have your fame greatly at heart and am trying to obtain recognition for your work.

This letter brought great comfort to Copernicus, who was still smarting under the spiteful blows of the burlesque. He showed the letter to Giese, who had been appointed Bishop of Kulm in Prussia. He had suffered an attack of malaria and Copernicus, as Giese's physician, had been summoned to his bedside. After Giese's health was restored, the medical visit developed into a

136

summer holiday—the first vacation Copernicus had taken in many years.

Copernicus had taken along his scholarly visitor, Rheticus, the young Protestant who, in spite of his Lutheran faith, remained deeply devoted to his Catholic teacher. Copernicus, Giese and Rheticus discussed Cardinal von Schoenberg's letter as they strolled through the gardens of the Kulm Cathedral. "The cardinal is right," said Giese. "You owe it to the world and yourself to publish the results of your investigations as soon as possible."

"But I am not yet through with my investigations," replied Copernicus, "and thus far my book hasn't advanced beyond the first few chapters."

"I agree with my friend," nodded Rheticus. "It takes many years to graft new fruits upon the tree of knowledge. Especially when the superstitious adversaries, like a horde of unruly children, keep throwing stones at the fruit."

"And also," added Copernicus with a grim smile, "when they are intent upon destroying the gardener along with his garden."

"I am quite aware of all this," observed Giese. "But let us be practical, Nicolas. We are not growing younger. What if something should happen to you before the book is finished?"

"I have often thought of that, my friend, so I am doing my best to stay alive. Simple food, plenty of exercise, no exciting diversions and no bad habits. And—let me confess—a healthy respect for those who might burn me if I expressed my thoughts too openly or too soon. I know that some people might blame me for this caution. Perhaps I am a coward. It's hard for us to look within ourselves and explain the real motives for our actions, but I don't believe it is fear that compels me to be so cautious. It is rather the passion to be absolutely right. Believe me, my friends, I value truth much more dearly than I value my life."

"I believe you," said Giese.

"Moreover," Copernicus went on, "if I should die before my work is finished, Rheticus will complete it. I keep in close touch with him at every step. I have explained to him all my astronomical observations, mathematical calculations, the tables of planetary orbits, the measures of time and space comprehended within these orbits, and the scientific conclusions that are to be based upon the findings I have accumulated throughout the years."

Rheticus nodded. "Should the work be left for me to finish, which God forbid, I would do my best. It would not be the great book of Copernicus, of course, but at least it would be a reflection of his light." Turning to his teacher, he added, "A very poor reflection, I'm afraid. So you had better stay alive and do the job yourself."

"I have every intention of doing so," laughed Copernicus, "even though I have the utmost faith in your ability. But to return to Cardinal von Schoenberg's letter. I am planning to incorporate it into my book. I will show the world that my ideas are not contrary to religion when they can appeal to the mind of a man so high in the government of the Church."

"It is the business of religion," observed Rheticus, "to be always on the side of the truth."

As the summer wore on, the three friends returned again and again to the subject of Copernicus' book. "You have told me," said Giese, "that you have already written the first few chapters. Do you mind giving me a summary of them?"

"I would rather not, Tiedemann. A small tidbit can hardly give you the relish of the entire meal. I may rewrite those chapters or even omit them as the work progresses. As a matter of fact, I have not even decided upon a title for the book. Perhaps you and Rheticus can supply the title when you see the entire manuscript."

"I have already suggested a title," said Rheticus. "*The Great Revolution.* The book, you see, will represent a double revolution—in the motions of the stars and in the current of human thought."

"Let us be modest," Copernicus said gently, "and stick to one revolution at a time. Suppose we confine ourselves to the heavens and let the current of human thought pursue its own course."

"I have the title!" exclaimed Giese. *The Revolution of the Heavens.*"

"No," objected Rheticus. "That sounds too much like an account of the battles among the Greek gods on Olympus."

"What about calling it *A Journey through the Heavens?*" said Giese.

"Aren't we a bit premature?" Copernicus suggested. "Why not wait for the arrival of the baby before we give it a name?"

There the matter was left for the time. Giese and Rheticus continued to search for a title, while Copernicus went ahead with his study of the stars.

As before, he met interruptions—the displeasure of Dantiscus, the new Bishop of Ermland, the degradation of one of his closest friends, Sculteti, and his increasing duties as a physician. "The troubles of the earth," he observed sadly to Rheticus, "are always conspiring to divert my attention from the contemplation of the heavens."

140

Chapter 13

As NEW BISHOP at Frauenburg, Dantiscus had entered upon a personal crusade against what he called "the subversive propaganda" of Copernicus. Unable to punish him in person, he tried to attack him through his housekeeper, a Polish girl with an infectious smile and a generous heart. Insisting that she was too attractive a person for the household of a church canon, Dantiscus issued several orders to Copernicus to dismiss her. But a good housekeeper was not easy to get and Copernicus found one excuse after another for ignoring his superior's command.

The bishop hated to be disobeyed. He did not think it wise to quarrel outright with the nephew and protégé of the late great Bishop Watzelrode, but he imposed all sorts of menial tasks upon him. Copernicus accepted these tasks without complaint, for he had no wish to provoke an open quarrel with the bishop. He answered politely even when Dantiscus kept inquiring in acid tones what progress he was making in his efforts to stop the sun. "I am trying to do my best," he said, "both as a servant of the Church and as a student of God's divine plan."

For Dantiscus, who was an ardent believer in astrology, any attempt to overthrow it was almost as great a heresy as a conspiracy to abolish religion. Furthermore, he believed that Copernicus was unfaithful to the Catholic Church because of his tolerance toward members of other churches. The bishop was especially irked at the friendship between Copernicus and Rheticus, whose frequent visits to Frauenburg he denounced as "the incursions of Satan into the Holy Land."

At times Dantiscus tried to give "fatherly advice"—as he expressed it—to his "erring son," Copernicus. He told him frankly that there could be no promotion in the

Church for a Catholic who associated with Lutherans, or who tried to overthrow old beliefs either in theology or in science.

"Let us be honest with each other, Copernicus. You are a brilliant, dedicated and energetic man—just the type we need for our Church leaders. With your talent, background and personality you could become a bishop —perhaps even a cardinal. But you are devoted to the wrong causes. You are meddling with the secrets of God's creation and you are hobnobbing with the enemies of the True Church. Take my advice, my son. Give up your useless preoccupation with the stars. Renounce your atheistic friends. If you will listen to my friendly warning, dismiss that flirtatious housekeeper of yours. Remove these obstructions from your path and I can give you my personal assurance that you will travel far beyond your present position."

"But, Your Reverence, I have little desire for ecclesiastical advancement. My personal taste lies in other directions. I prefer to labor in obscurity. I can do my work best in silence. The glamour of high office would only distract my attention from my more important task."

"And that is?"

"To add my little grain of observation to the slowly accumulated knowledge of the world."

"You are an unusual man, Copernicus. A scholar of

143

extraordinary talent—yet with no ambition, no desire for glory, no passion to make your mark upon your own generation."

"I suppose you are right. I can't explain it, but that is how I feel. It seems that I am one of those people born to instruct the future rather than to dazzle the present."

"Even at your personal sacrifice?"

"It is no sacrifice for me to pursue my work. I assure you it gives me the greatest satisfaction."

"But suppose your studies lead you to no definite end? Suppose the goal you are trying to reach turns out to be a mirage?"

"It is still wonderful to have made the attempt. Besides, I have done enough work to know that I am going in the right direction."

"God forbid!" cried the bishop in all sincerity. It was the nature of Dantiscus to defend the old, just as it was the nature of Copernicus to explore the new. Yet both of them were equally convinced that they had truth on their side.

"Perhaps it is part of God's plan," as Copernicus once remarked to Giese, "to balance the search and the obstruction in such a way that only a little knowledge at a time can be parceled out to the human race. The world, as I see it, is like a play in which every generation represents a new scene and a little advance in the devel-

144

opment of the plot. What would be the fun of watching the play if we could see the entire story in the first act?"

At any rate, Dantiscus was active among the forces of obstruction. He did everything in his power to thwart the astonomer and to inflame the minds of the other canons against him. Many of them, in their effort to curry favor with their superior, kept irritating Copernicus with petty annoyances or else left him severely alone.

Dantiscus would have liked to get Copernicus out of the way altogether, but that was impossible—especially when the ideas of Copernicus had not as yet been published and therefore there was little direct evidence against him.

In addition to his campaign against Copernicus' housekeeper, Dantiscus found other ways to strike at him indirectly. He began to persecute some of his intimate friends, especially singling out Sculteti, who, next to Giese and Rheticus, was one of Copernicus' most ardent admirers. Dantiscus accused Sculteti of heresy. Copernicus sent a letter to the Pope in defense of his friend, but to no avail. The Pope listened to his bishop, and Sculteti was expelled from the cathedral and hounded out of Poland.

Thus Copernicus, as he grew older, was becoming more and more neglected and alone. The friends of his youth were dying off, and the men who took their places knew little, and cared even less, about the aging stargazer whom their bishop regarded with utter contempt.

There was one channel for Copernicus' activity which even Dantiscus was compelled to respect—his skill as a physician, especially when Dantiscus himself suffered a series of fainting spells.

Dantiscus had a brilliant mind as well as a surly temper. He frowned upon the ignorance of most of the doctors of his period, who knew practically nothing about the human body and applied the same treatment to almost every ailment. He was familiar with "medicinal" concoctions made of such items as stewed bats, powdered animal horns, roots and barks of trees, melted jewels, toadskins, vipers' lungs, spider webs and even more unsavory medicines such as goat's blood and dung. Dantiscus knew that Copernicus would have nothing to do with these distasteful potions, and trusted the advanced medical knowledge of his canon just as he feared his advanced astronomical theories. He had observed Copernicus' treatment of the other members of the cathedral and he approved of it. His predecessor, Bishop Ferber, had suffered from frequent attacks of colic and gout. Copernicus had always helped Ferber during those attacks.

146

Dantiscus also realized that the scholarly canon was not the type of man to let his personal feelings interfere with his medical work. Therefore, when he took sick, he felt no hesitation in calling upon Copernicus. But Copernicus was somewhat reluctant to treat Dantiscus and spoke freely about it to his patient.

"I would rather you summoned another doctor. Not that I wouldn't do my best, Your Reverence. A doctor's first duty, you know, is to his patient. But perhaps, without knowing it, our deep-seated political and scientific differences might interfere with my judgment. I say this not for my sake but for yours. I think you might be better in other hands."

In spite of this warning, however, Dantiscus insisted upon retaining the services of Copernicus. And in his anxiety to avoid any involuntary lapse on his own part, Copernicus took double care with his patient. He wrote to the court physician of the Polish king describing the bishop's symptoms and asking for his advice as to the value of his own prescribed treatment. In those days of difficult travel, it was customary for doctors to communicate by letter instead of calling one another in for consultations. The court physician made a minor suggestion or two, but on the whole approved of Copernicus' treatment. Dantiscus, thanks to the devoted care he received, grew gradually better.

One day during his convalescence Dantiscus thanked Copernicus for his devotion. "Of course you realize," he said, "that you are treating a dangerous foe. When I get well, I shall resume my opposition to your work. I shall keep on trying my best to have you excommunicated."

"I understand, Your Reverence."

"I may even be the instrument of your imprisonment or death."

"I know."

A smile of admiration broke through the hostility of Dantiscus. "You amaze me, Copernicus. And yet, were I in your place, I would do exactly the same."

"I am sure you would, Your Reverence. But please don't excite yourself now. Our main concern at present is for you to get well."

In due time Dantiscus recovered from his illness. He returned to his persecution of Copernicus, and Copernicus returned to his book. Each of them was determined to be true to his appointed task.

148

Chapter 14

DANTISCUS FINALLY drove Copernicus to dismiss his
housekeeper, but this was not the end of the bishop's
hostility. Dantiscus, the son of a Danzig brewer, had
become a bishop through ability and perseverance and
had set himself up as a leader of the opposition against
the Protestants. He was especially irked at Copernicus'
tolerance toward them. "I am determined," he declared,
"to bring these apostates back to the Church or else to
the stake!"

Dantiscus also disliked Copernicus for his "too great kindness"—as he put it—toward the peasants. When their taxes fell due and they were unable to pay them, Copernicus was inclined to be lenient with them. "Let us wait," he said. "These people are very poor and their taxes are too high."

But Dantiscus was adamant. "It is your business as my representative," he insisted, "to collect the taxes when due and to accept no excuses!"

This matter became another constant source of irritation between the two men. Dantiscus called the astronomer a rebel not only against learning but against all the laws of his country and his Church. Copernicus, however, replied that he was merely trying to live up to the teaching of the Prophets—to do justice, to love mercy, and to walk humbly with God. "Let us not forget," he said quietly, "that our Lord, also, was merciful to the poor."

Dantiscus employed spies to watch Copernicus in the hope that his subordinate "might betray such heresies as would bring him into the power of the Inquisition."

But Copernicus kept his peace, although it was one of the most difficult periods of his life. He was practically ostracized from the people among whom he lived. His relationship to the late Bishop Watzelrode had by this time been largely forgotten. His actions and even his thoughts were suspect. He was no longer young. His strength had begun to fail. And his superior kept scrutinizing and criticizing his work in the Church as well as his observation of the stars.

Copernicus realized that the bishop was trying to atone for a somewhat doubtful past, for he had once looked with tolerance upon the Protestants. He had even visited Luther, whom he had described as "keen, learned, eloquent—in short, a good companion." Now Dantiscus was punishing in Copernicus "the weakness of forbearance" to which he himself had yielded in his earlier years. Having committed an error, as he believed, he atoned for it by punishing others who were committing the same error. "There is no severer judge," Copernicus remarked to Giese, "than a reformed sinner."

Copernicus did not regard his attitude toward the peasants or the Lutherans as a special virtue or a special sin. Looking upon himself as dispassionately as possible, he felt that he had been sent into the world not to quarrel but to teach. All he asked was to be left alone with his thoughts. However, he bowed patiently before the storm of persecution just as a plant would bow before the onslaught of the wind. He submitted to the orders of Dantiscus concerning his religious duties but went quietly ahead with his studies. When his disciple

151

Rheticus came to Frauenburg for another visit, they again discussed his book, which was now almost completed.

"I will see to its publication as soon as it is ready," said Rheticus.

"I shall be grateful for the favor," replied Copernicus. "I am getting too old to look after such matters myself."

Rheticus nodded. "Yes. You have spent a lifetime on this one book."

"Not quite a lifetime," smiled Copernicus. "Only twenty years."

"Long enough," said his young friend. "And now it is time to publish it."

"Not yet. I still have to revise it and eliminate any possible errors. The planets, as you well know, do not always seem to keep in their proper orbits. To be sure, they behave much more regularly in my system than they do in the Ptolemaic system, but there is one point that still bothers me. I still do not understand why the retrograde motion of Mars is not always identical. It varies little from year to year."

"I wish I could give you the answer," said Rheticus.

But neither of them could find the answer. Copernicus, however, was determined to withhold the publication of his book in an effort to straighten out the difficulty. "I may need another ten years, in addition to the twenty I have already spent, in order to make my calculations as accurate as possible."

"Thirty years on a single book!" exclaimed Rheticus.

"All important matters take time. It took several hundred years, you know, for the Ten Commandments to develop into the Sermon on the Mount."

"But you are sixty now. In another ten years you will be too old to enjoy the fruits of your labor."

"My greatest joy in planting is not to pluck my own fruits but to provide them for others."

Rheticus looked earnestly at his master. "I understand exactly what you mean. You are the most modest and the most unselfish man I have ever met."

His closest friend, Tiedemann Giese, urged him to be more emphatic in the spreading of his ideas. "The only way to be heard," he insisted, "is to make a noise."

But Copernicus shook his head. "The voice of reason is heard, not in the thunder or the whirlwind, but in the quieter moments of life. Noise is painful, you know, and people try to forget it as soon as possible after it subsides."

Rheticus, who was present at the time of this conversation, agreed with Copernicus. "I believe you are right," he said. "Today a man like Dantiscus creates a big stir because he makes a big noise. But those who live the longest in the memory of mankind are the prophets and the thinkers and the saints—the men of the still, small voice and the vision of God. I dare say that in the coming generations Dantiscus will live only in the reflected glory of Copernicus. He will be remembered merely as the foolish oppressor of a great and wise man."

"Thank you for your generous words." Copernicus smiled. "But I am sure you place too high a value upon my simple labor."

"The whole world," cried Rheticus, "will someday agree with me about your greatness!"

"That," chuckled Copernicus, "remains to be seen. And since neither you nor I will be here to see it, suppose we forget about our future stature and concentrate upon our present task."

The world was still engulfed in a turmoil of further battles between the Catholics and the Protestants, struggles between the Germans and the French, conflicts between the Hungarians and the Turks, a breach between King Henry VIII of England and the Pope, a whirlpool of dissensions between different countries and between discordant factions within every country. Copernicus, who had never lost his interest in the affairs of the world, took an active part in several of the plans for settling the various disputes, his constant effort being, if at all possible, to bring order out of chaos.

He was always glad, however, to look away from the disorders of the earth into the order of the heavens. He prepared a table of sunrises and sunsets and computed the length of the year; he designed a number of sundials to be used in Frauenburg, Allenstein and Torún; he discussed with other scholars the nature of the comets that had appeared in Europe within the past twenty-five years; and he worked incessantly on his intricate computations of planetary movements. These computations, as he explained to those who were interested in seeing them, were too difficult for the layman to understand. "Only a person skilled in astronomy and trained in higher mathematics will be able to follow them." Indeed, he pointed out, his book was mathematical rather than astronomical.

"Yet in general," he said, "my work will establish two important facts: first, that the earth moves around the sun; and second, that a single universal law can account for the motions of the earth and of all the heavenly bodies."

This much he disclosed to the more educated people who wanted to know about his work. As for the rabble who laughed at his stargazing habits, he merely smiled at their ignorance. Rheticus, who was less patient with the stupidity of the masses, had a biting phrase to express his contempt. *"Quod licet Jovi non licet bovi,"* It is not for the clod to see the ways of God. But Copernicus upbraided his young friend for his attitude. "Let us not be too hard on the ignorant masses," he said. "They never asked to be born either stupid or poor."

His heart always went out to those people. He shut his eyes to their prejudices, forgave them for their improvidence and continued to help them in their sickness. Although, to the people of Ermland, his astronomical study was a subject for ridicule, his medical knowledge was ground for respect. He had the "healing touch." He was regarded as a leader among the physicians of his day. "The masses," wrote Giese in one of his letters to Rheticus, "worship him as a godlike being who examines them when they are sick, personally prepares the herbs he uses for his drugs, and refuses pay for his services." Other people wrote similar letters full of praise for the "wonder doctor of Frauenburg."

Copernicus treated both his friends and his enemies with equal solicitude. In addition to Danticus, whom he had attended on several occasions, he once received a request from Duke Albrecht to come to the bedside of his favorite counselor, Georg von Kunheim. Copernicus had bitter memories about the duke, the former leader of the Teutonic Knights who had attacked him at the

156

Castle of Allenstein. And Kunheim had been Albrecht's chief adviser at the time. Yet Copernicus had not a moment's hesitation. Though well along in his sixties, he traveled by carriage from Frauenburg to the "distant foreign land" of Prussia in order to help a fellow creature in distress.

Duke Albrecht, who was made of coarser clay than Copernicus, continued to poke fun at the astronomer though he respected him as a physician. One day, as Albrecht's court astrologer was trying to explain the theory of Copernicus, the duke called out to the servant who was carrying the wine jug to the guests: "Watch out and don't spill it!" When the servant looked at him in surprise, he added, "The jug, you know, is spinning together with the rest of the earth around the sun!"

Then, turning to his guests, Albrecht declared that he took the theory of Copernicus as a personal insult. "How dare this man allege," he shouted, "that I, the Grand Master of Prussia, am nothing but an insect whirling around the sky on a little pellet of mud!"

When this outburst was reported to Copernicus, he shrugged his shoulders and smiled. "The Duke is a fortunate man. His journey through space is free of all unnecessary burdens. He has such a light little head to carry on his shoulders."

That night, as he pondered upon the arrogance of

Duke Albrecht, he wrote on the flyleaf of one of his books:

> Most of our arrogance, including my own, is due to our ignorance. And most of our ignorance is due to the brevity of our life. We die when we have just begun to learn, and before we have had a chance to evaluate our own little contribution to the wisdom of the world.

He dried the words with a sprinkling of sand over the page and turned back to his studies. His "own little contribution" to the world's wisdom was almost finished. He had charted across the heavens a course never known to any other man. And, God willing, he would point out this course to the world before he died. Let others who came after him evaluate the work. It was enough for him to have served as the guide.

Chapter 15

FOR TWO YEARS, from 1539 to 1541, Rheticus was the constant companion of Copernicus. It was dangerous for a Lutheran and a Catholic to meet and exchange views, yet the two were willing to face the risk for the further advancement of science.

Rheticus had brought Copernicus a number of scientific books, including a Latin edition of Euclid's *Geometry* and a Greek edition of Ptolemy's *Almagest*—his famous work on astronomy. Copernicus was grateful for the gift. His own editions of these books had become tattered through constant thumbing. "I don't read many books," he explained, "only the best. And these I examine so often that I keep wearing them out. One of my most precious books," he added, "is the *Almagest*."

"I, too, share your reverence for Ptolemy," Rheticus told him. "His work is like the Old Testament of astronomy. The book you are now writing, I am convinced, will be accepted as the New Testament."

"Not the New Testament, my friend, merely a restatement of the ideas that have been forgotten for centuries. I am only recalling—and trying to prove—the theories of Pythagoras, Philolaus and Aristarchus. Even among the more recent astronomers I am not the first to accept these views. The Jewish philosopher and physician Maimonides disagreed with the geocentric theory of Ptolemy, objecting, as I myself object, that his system reveals many inaccuracies in the Celestial Time Clock, as if God Himself were subject to error. This, too, was the objection of some of the Arabian scientists in the thirteenth century. And just before our own generation Cardinal Nicolas of Cusa declared that, in his opinion, the earth definitely moves. Like a majestic king, the sun refuses to go around visiting his subjects, but sits on his throne while his subjects come to pay their respects to him."

"A pretty figure of speech," observed Rheticus, "and —as you have proved at least to *my* satisfaction—correct. But this brings me to the subject we have discussed again and again. Are you ready to publish your book?"

"I really can't say. I'm almost seventy now, and the book is still far from complete."

"No scientific study is *ever* complete," objected Rheticus.

"True enough. But I am not at all certain that my observations are absolutely correct. In the first place, it takes not years but decades to verify a slight movement of a star among the complicated motions of all the other stars. In the second place, my instruments are so inadequate. A sundial, a gnomon, a Jacob's staff—hardly anything more. Just a few sticks nailed together into triangles and squares for computing the infinite dimensions of the universe."

"If only our eyes could be enlarged to see more clearly and deeply into the mysteries of the sky!" exclaimed Rheticus.

"Someday, perhaps, an instrument may be invented to enlarge our vision. But for the present we must depend upon our imperfect eyesight. This brings me to another reason for withholding my book—the imperfection

161

of my vision, especially in this country which is almost always shrouded in a mist. Fortune did not give me, as it gave Ptolemy, the opportunity to watch the cloudless skies of Alexandria. The Nile does not breathe fogs as does our Vistula. Here the stars are too frequently hidden from sight."

"Nevertheless you have performed a miracle with the inner vision of mathematics to supplement the imperfect outer vision of the eyes. You have called upon your imagination to help your senses, and upon your reason to bolster your imagination. After examining your book with the utmost care, I am convinced that, even in its present form, it is accurate enough to bring a new revelation to the world."

"Yet I still hesitate. That erratic motion of Mars is still unexplained." He drew a diagram of the orbit of Mars as conceived in his astronomical system. "Note how this planet describes a circle around the sun not in a simple line but in a series of loops—as if spinning back upon itself every now and then."

Rheticus nodded. "Yes, but this is just one possible error in a book that is otherwise correct. And your main thesis—the recognition that the earth moves around the sun—is the key that will help later astronomers to unlock the mystery of the heavens and to explain even the seemingly erratic movement of Mars."

162

"I quite agree with you," said Copernicus. "And yet the great majority of the people look upon my ideas as absurd."

"That is because they haven't read them. People have a garbled notion of your theory as it passes from mouth to mouth. You owe it to the world to publish the book so that your ideas will be available at first hand."

Copernicus smiled wryly. "I daresay that the book, if published, wouldn't reach the sale of a thousand copies."

"Not at first perhaps. But in time your ideas will be known to the entire world."

"You're an optimist," laughed Copernicus, "and you almost convince me." But he told Rheticus that his eyes were bothering him and his general health was poor. He claimed that he was too old and feeble to see his manuscript through the press.

But Rheticus reassured him on that point. "I will myself look after the publication," he said. "I have a friend, Johannes Petrejus, in Nürnberg who is interested in issuing scientific books. As a matter of fact, I have already written to him about your work. He is very eager to see the manuscript."

"Well, I don't know . . ." said Copernicus. But the very tone in which he spoke the words indicated that he was on the point of yielding.

At last Rheticus hit upon a bold idea that compelled

his teacher to take the final step. He decided to write a review of Copernicus' book before the book itself was published, and entitle it "The First Account of the Revolutions of the Spheres."

He prepared the review in the form of a letter to Johann Schöner, one of his former teachers at Nürnberg:

My learned master Copernicus desires nothing better than to follow in the footsteps of the divine Ptolemy, Father of Astronomy. Yet, having before his eyes the observations of all ages together with his own, he has assembled the facts in his mind as in a catalog. He has accepted whatever makes sense and rejected whatever does not make sense; and thus he has developed a new, true and complete picture of the universe.

In this new picture, the universe is like a musical instrument whose strings are so adjusted to the other strings that all of them together produce a perfect melody without a single discord. Or, to use another figure, the universe is like a clock in which every wheel occupies its proper place and performs its prescribed rotation for the harmonious precision of the whole . . .

Owing to the scarcity of astronomical instruments, my master was like a blind man who, with only a staff to guide him, must make a great, endless, hazardous journey that winds through innumerable, lonely places. Often he found himself alone, desolate, and on the verge of despair. But at last the Lord, in His compassion, stretched forth His hand and guided him to the desired goal.

Hence I am bold to declare that my master's astronomy can be justly called eternal and to predict that it will be confirmed by the observations of posterity throughout the centuries.

The review, which appeared in pamphlet form, created a sensation among scholars. Such high praise from so eminent an authority as Rheticus whetted their interest in the new book. People wrote to Copernicus, asking for copies in the belief that it had already been published. Copernicus was at last persuaded to publish his book and Rheticus left for Germany to submit the manuscript to his publisher friend, Petrejus. He took one copy along with him and made a second copy which he sent to Tiedemann Giese. Copernicus kept the original, which was all marked up with annotations and corrections. Thus far no title had been selected for the book.

At Rheticus' departure Copernicus felt, as he expressed it, "bereft of the use of my right hand." Among the canons of Frauenburg there was only one young man, George Donner, who dared to show any concern for him. All the others, submitting to the orders of

Dantiscus, stayed away from the "heretical astronomer" as from a plague. Copernicus was almost totally blind now. The constant vigils in the fogs of Poland had taken their toll.

In the autumn of 1542 Copernicus fell seriously ill. He suffered a hemorrhage and had to take to his bed. Giese, hearing of the illness, wrote a letter to Donner:

> I know that Copernicus has always counted you among his truest friends. I pray, therefore, that you will stand by him and take care of the great and lonely man whom you, with me, have ever loved. Let him not be deprived of our brotherly help in his distress, and let us not prove ungrateful to a friend who has so richly deserved our gratitude and love.

Donner attended Copernicus in his last painful days. The hemorrhage was followed by a partial paralysis, so that the astronomer was hardly able to speak. Occasionally he whispered to his young attendant, "Have you heard from Rheticus? Any news about my book?"

But news was scant. Rheticus, too, had a hard road to travel. Many of his former friends neglected him because of his own "heresy." It was a serious matter, in those days of bitter religious controversy, for a Protestant to sponsor a book by a Catholic.

After submitting the book to Petrejus, Rheticus was unable to see it through the press. He had been dismissed from his teaching job at the University of Wittenberg. Appointed to a similar post at Leipzig University, he was too busy with his new duties to attend to the exacting details of publication. He handed the task over to a Nürnberg friend of his, Andrew Osiander—a Lutheran clergyman who did not share the general intolerance of his colleagues toward the Catholics.

Rheticus believed that he could trust Osiander, but he was mistaken. Though tolerant toward the Catholics, Osiander was afraid to associate himself with a book that might be condemned by the religious extremists on both sides of the fence. And so he decided to discuss the matter with Petrejus.

"The book," he said to the publisher, "is based upon a dangerous idea. It will shatter the traditions of the centuries and the very foundations of the world as we know it."

Petrejus nodded. "I have no doubt of it."

"And it may bury you and me, along with the author, in the ruins."

"I, for one, am willing to take the risk. For I believe the book tells the truth."

"I am not so sure of it. Yet I do admit that the author's arguments are ingenious."

"Perhaps you'd like to withdraw from the project? In that case I would ask Rheticus to suggest another editor."

Osiander hesitated. To wash his hands of the book might save him considerable trouble, perhaps even persecution. But on the other hand, his editorial contribution to the new theory might possibly mean eternal fame. It was a difficult choice to make.

A sudden idea struck him. "Suppose," he suggested to Petrejus, "you allow me to write an introduction to the book. In it I would state that Copernicus has advanced his new picture of the universe not as an actual fact but as a working hypothesis. In other words, I would implant in the reader's mind the notion that Copernicus himself was not sure of his theory, but proposed it merely as an abstract mathematical formula for computing the positions of the spheres."

"But would that be quite honest?"

"Why not? Can anyone be sure that he is absolutely right? Moreover, Copernicus has dedicated his book to the Pope. I submit that an author who seeks sanction from the head of his Church should be more humble in his scientific approach. He should use the modest suggestion 'I believe,' rather than the arrogant assertion 'I declare.'"

Petrejus reluctantly agreed to Osiander's plan. Thus a fraud was perpetrated not only upon Copernicus, who was too ill to attend to the publication himself, but also upon the general public. Copernicus had written an introduction to the book, but when the book came off the press, it contained the additional introduction by Osiander. Since the second one was not signed, the reader was allowed the impression that Copernicus had written both of them.

The two introductions were utterly inconsistent. The first one boldly declared that the book was a true picture of the universe; the second one cautiously hinted that it was nothing more than a cunning supposition to help people solve a few astronomical problems.

When the book came out, Rheticus and Tiedemann Giese recognized the deception immediately and were furious about it, but the general reading public failed to see either the inconsistency or the fraud. It took the world almost a hundred years to realize that Copernicus actually meant what he said when he declared that the earth moves around the sun.

As for Copernicus himself, he had almost completely lost his memory by the time the book was published. He was no longer able to accuse Osiander or to feel any hurt. Nor could he enjoy the praise of the few who really understood. The book fell like a feather upon a silent sea. There was no advance payment from the publisher; there were no royalties. A few copies were sent to Giese and Rheticus, and one copy was given to Copernicus as he lay at the point of death.

Giese came to visit Copernicus just before the end, and it was he who brought the first printed copy of the book to him. The publisher had given it a title, *De revolutionibus orbium coelestium, Concerning the Revolutions of the Heavenly Spheres.* Copernicus was unable to see the book, but he held it in his hands and began feebly to thumb the leaves. Giese could not be sure that Copernicus knew he was holding his own precious book.

"It is your life's work, master," he said gently.

A faint smile passed over the dying man's face. He managed to whisper a few words with his final breath: "My work—the stars!"

Copernicus was laid to rest at the Frauenburg Cathedral, but no memorial was set up to mark the date of his death, May 24, 1543. Recognition of Copernicus was a slow process—even his burial place was forgotten for a time. It was not until thirty-eight years later, in 1581, that a memorial tablet was set up on one of the cathedral walls. Even this tablet was removed in the eighteenth century to make room for the epitaph of a bishop whose name was regarded as more important than that of Copernicus, who had been a mere canon. The first monument to Copernicus was erected at his birthplace, the city of Torún, three centuries after his death.

Chapter 16

In his dedication of *Revolutions,* Copernicus called astronomy a "more divine than human science." He went on to praise the "understanding and exactitude" of Ptolemy, who "had brought this science almost to perfection." But, insisted Copernicus, "we see many things which do not tally with what should have taken place according to this theory." And so, Copernicus declared, "I admit openly that my teaching is in many ways entirely different from that of Ptolemy."

171

He then proceeded to explain the differences between the two theories. According to the Ptolemaic system the universe consisted of about ten thousand concentric circles—that is, circles having the same center. That center was the earth—firm, immovable, enthroned as the ruler of the moon and the sun and the stars. All the heavenly bodies rotated around the earth in their circular paths, paying their obeisance to the earth and producing the music of the spheres.

Copernicus agreed with Ptolemy that the universe is an enormous sphere of matter and space. The sphere, he claimed, is the perfect form of nature, using the raindrop as an illustration. The entire universe, he said, behaves like a single drop of water. Whatever distortions it may assume under stress, it finally returns to, and remains in, its spherical form. Thus every star and planet within the universe, like the universe itself, is a sphere.

Copernicus overthrew the Ptolemaic theory of the universe when he stated that the earth moves around the sun, even though it *appears* that the sun moves from east to west around the earth.

The trouble with Ptolemy, as Copernicus saw it, was that he had examined the heavens from the earth as if it were a *stationary* platform. But if, Copernicus declared, the earth itself is a *moving* platform, the motions

172

that we observe in the sky are not *absolute* but *relative* motions—that is, relative to the motions of the earth.

The ancient astronomers, in other words, had acted as if they were observers of a horse race from a seat in the grandstand. But the modern astronomer, thanks to Copernicus, realizes that he is one of the riders in a horse race observing the motions and the relative positions of all the horses, including his own, while his own horse is galloping along with the others.

Ptolemy had declared that if the earth rotated on its own axis nothing would rise or fall in a straight line. He had also argued that "if the earth whirled around at tremendous speeds, it would necessarily fly to pieces." In that case, Copernicus pointed out, the whole sky would have to make a complete revolution around the earth every twenty-four hours in order to make the stars rise and set every night. And, since the sphere of the sky is so much greater than that of the earth, the speed of its revolution would also have to be much greater. Copernicus concluded that it made more sense to ascribe a comparatively slow motion to the tiny earth rather than a stupendously rapid motion to the infinite sky. As he said, he rejected the Ptolemaic system because it made neither aesthetic nor mathematical sense. The sun stands still and the earth moves, he said, because "the condition of firmness and immobility is considered more noble and divine than the condition of instability and motion."

And what could be more noble or more divine than the sun? "The Greeks called it the guide and soul of the world; Sophocles spoke of it as the All-seeing One; Trismegistus held it to be the visible embodiment of God. Now, therefore," declared Copernicus, "let us place the sun upon a royal throne, let it in truth guide the circling family of planets, including the earth."

There was another aesthetic consideration that led Copernicus to his heliocentric theory. God, he maintained, governs the entire universe in accordance with a single, simple law. By placing the sun in the center, Copernicus was able to reduce the ten thousand different celestial circles of Ptolemy to one single system of planets rotating around the sun.

For, declared Copernicus, the other planets are likewise carried along "the highways of the heavens" around the central star known to us as the sun. And all these motions are the result of the infallible and unchangeable but simple law of nature. Each planet revolves in its own orbit around the sun, never deviating from its appointed path. Every season arrives at its appointed time, and every heavenly body fulfills its appointed destiny.

In his book Copernicus then attempted to prove mathematically that his theory was correct. His computations were rather involved and, owing to his assumption of circular orbits for the planets, they were frequently incorrect. Nevertheless, they succeeded in establishing a system that was much closer to the truth.

The uniformity that Copernicus sought he did not find. Kepler, however, corrected the error by establishing proof of the elliptical planetary orbits and thus filling in the gaps in the Copernican theory.

Chapter 17

COPERNICUS' GREAT BOOK, like his name, was neglected for a long time. Only a few copies of the first edition were sold. Here and there a reader became converted to his heliocentric picture of the heavens, but the masses still adhered to their old belief that the earth was the throne of the universe.

Among the earliest converts to the Copernican system was an English schoolmaster, Robert Recorde. In

1556, thirteen years after the death of Copernicus, Recorde wrote a book on astronomy entitled *The Castle
of Knowledge.* In it he explained that he had read the
work of Copernicus, which, having been written in
Latin, was available to scholars of various countries. His
own work, he said, was written in English so that the
intelligent layman might be able to read it. The book
was a sort of "Astronomy Made Easy." It mentioned the
theory of Copernicus, "a man of great learning, of
much experience and of wonderful diligence in observation, who hath declared that the Earth moveth cir-
cularly about his own center . . . If you are inclined
to ridicule the idea," the author of *The Castle of Knowledge* cautioned his reader, "you must be careful to condemn nothing which you do not well understand. Someday," he predicted, "you will be as earnest to credit [the
idea of Copernicus] as you are now to condemn it."

And thus some of the first seeds of the new astronomy
were planted among the general readers of England.

Another early convert to the Copernican system was
Giordano Bruno, born in Naples five years after the
death of Copernicus. He became a Dominican priest;
later he revolted against the doctrines of the Church.
Compelled to flee from Italy, he became a wandering
teacher and ardent disciple of Copernicus.

But he went far beyond Copernicus in his denunciation of the orthodox teaching of his time. He declared that the sun was merely a star; that all the stars, indeed, were suns, each of them attended by a train of planets that moved around it as the earth moves around the sun. He further maintained that all the heavenly bodies were made of the same material, and that a great many of them were inhabited by creatures like ourselves.

He published these ideas in 1584, forty-one years after the printing of Copernicus' *Revolutions*. Bruno was living in England at the time, but became homesick for his native land. Shortly after his return to Italy he was arrested and brought to trial for his defiance against the faith. In 1600, after a long confinement in prison, he was burned at the stake. The chief charge against him was that he had attacked the religious beliefs of his day. His acceptance of the Copernican ideas was but a minor charge at his trial, yet Bruno's fate frightened the other adherents of Copernicus and checked the further teaching of his theory for a number of years.

But Copernicus had declared that he had the patience to wait beyond his own century.

It was in the following century that Copernicus' next two great disciples appeared—Johannes Kepler and Galileo Galilei. These two men were born only a few years after the death of Copernicus, but they produced their important works after 1600.

178

Johannes Kepler, a German scientist, had become acquainted with the Copernican system through Michael Maestlin, a professor at the University of Tübingen. This man had formerly served as a village pastor. Consumed with a passion for harmony, he tried to impress upon his students the idea of a single divine pattern that governed the motions of the stars in the heavens and the power of love on earth. He was a firm believer in Copernicus—"the reconciler of Heaven and Earth"—and he transmitted his belief to Kepler, who, at twenty-five, wrote his first book on the Copernican astronomy, *Mysterium cosmographicum, The Secret of the Universe.*

The book was but a sketchy outline of his later work, yet it brought down upon his head the denunciations of many of the leading scholars of the day. Kepler was not a man to accept blows without fighting back. Unlike Copernicus, he was quarrelsome, sarcastic and morose. His truculent manner as well as his scientific and religious beliefs brought about his exile from Germany. He took his family—a wife and six children—to Prague, where he became an assistant to Tycho Brahe, a famous astronomer who did not, however, fully accept the Copernican system.

Basing his work upon Tycho's extremely precise calculations of planetary orbits, Kepler was able to construct his laws of planetary motion, which clarified the Copernican theory. Copernicus had believed that the earth moves around the sun in a circular orbit. In his first law Kepler stated that the planet describes an *ellipse* rather than a circle. With the formulation of Kepler's three laws, it became possible for astronomers to calculate the location of every planet in relation to every other planet at every moment of time.

Kepler sent his books on astronomy to a few select people, one of them being the Italian scientist, Galileo Galilei. As soon as he read the preface to the first book, Galileo sent an enthusiastic letter to Kepler:

> I estimate myself happy to have as great an ally as you in my search for truth. I will read your work all the more willingly because I have for many years been a partisan of the Copernican view . . . I have collected many proofs of his view, but thus far I have not published them because I am deterred by the fate of our Teacher Copernicus who, though he had won immortal fame with a few, was condemned and ridiculed by the countless masses—for very great is the number of the stupid . . .

After constructing the first astronomical telescope Galileo was able to explore the heavens as no one had ever done before. The telescope—"the gazer into distant space"—was made possible by an accidental discovery of a Dutch optician, Hans Lippershey. One day Lippershey noticed that by placing a convex lens and a concave lens together he could bring distant objects closer. This phenomenon aroused the interest of Galileo, who made a scientific study of the subject, examining the curvatures and the groupings of various types of glasses and calculating the visual results.

In the summer of 1609 Galileo gave a public demonstration of the first scientifically constructed telescope in history. To an amazed crowd of friends and admirers he pointed out the miracles observed through his "magic magnifying glass." They beheld "sails and shipping . . . so far off that it was two hours before they could be seen with the naked eye. . . . And then at night, turning their gaze to the heavens, they beheld the nearness of the distant stars."

As a result of his own numerous observations through the telescope, Galileo wrote a book, *Sidereus nuncius, The Messenger of the Stars,* in which he reaffirmed the findings of Copernicus. "I give thanks to God," he wrote, "who has been pleased to show me, through my spyglass (*mio occhiale*), the greatest marvel of all—that the planets move around the sun."

Like Copernicus and the others who had dared to proclaim the new vision of the heavens, Galileo was persecuted for his ardent pursuit of scientific truth. "The unenlightened leaders," he declared, "work in accordance with a simple savage formula: If you can't refute, persecute. I believe that there is no greater hatred in the world than the hatred of ignorance against knowledge."

In 1633 Galileo was brought before the Inquisition and forced, under threat of death at the stake, to abjure his belief in a heliocentric universe. Old and sick and, in his own phrase, "more dead than alive," he was in no condition, physically or mentally, to defend himself.

"Before the Holy Gospels which I touch with my hands," he said, "I, Galileo Galilei, being seventy years of age and a prisoner on my knees, reject, curse and detest my former heresies . . . I now declare and swear that the earth does not move around the sun."

As he was being led, trembling and exhausted, away from the tribunal, he is said to have remarked under his breath, *"E pur si muove," "But the earth does move."*

After release from prison he was kept under house arrest and died in seclusion in 1642, a century after the death of Copernicus. Until the last, in spite of illness and blindness, Galileo actively continued his quest for knowledge.

The year of Galileo's death saw the birth of another great scientific figure—a man who would establish, once and for all, the validity of Copernicus' writings. Kepler had believed that the motion of the earth around the sun was the result of a force that pushed from behind; while Galileo, on the other hand, conjectured that the force pulled the earth. When Isaac Newton announced the law of universal gravitation in 1687, the issue was settled and the Copernican theory after about a hundred and fifty years, became widely accepted.

Newton's *Mathematical Principles of Natural Philosophy* "gathered all previous discoveries together"—to quote Copernicus' biographer, Hermann Kesten—"and laid the foundation for all future discoveries." In it he explained the motion of the earth as neither pushed nor pulled, but as an example of the type of force that all heavenly bodies exert on one another. Moreover, he stated that this force stems from a universal property of matter and that all bodies, from planets to particles, have a mutual attraction for one another—the strength of the attraction depending upon the masses of, and the distance between, the two bodies.

"Knowledge," Newton said, "is an accumulation of vision, the vision of the present added to that of the past." He acknowledged his debt to Copernicus as well as to Kepler and Galileo and others who had preceded him: "If I have seen farther, it is by standing on the shoulders of giants."

The giants of astronomy who came after Newton, each

of them standing upon the shoulders of his predecessors, were able to penetrate still further into the mysteries of the universe: Oleus Römer, Edmund Halley, Sir William Herschel, Simon Newcomb, Sir Arthur Eddington, Sir James Jeans and Albert Einstein—to mention a few.

By choosing the heliocentric notion of the universe, Copernicus was able to provide a theory that satisfactorily answered certain questions about the motions of heavenly bodies. It also provided the key to later discoveries, made by men who were equally dedicated to the search for scientific truth, regardless of personal jeopardy. Far from belittling human dignity, the Copernican theory has whetted man's intellectual appetite; it has given wings to his aspirations and dreams.

Today's leaps and thrusts into space far surpass anything that yesterday's astronomers could have imagined. Tomorrow's journeys through the universe will be the ultimate proof of man's awakening from the earth-bound sleep that Copernicus was the first to disturb.

Bibliography

Alter, Dinsmore. *Pictorial Astronomy*. New York: Thomas Y. Crowell Company, 1956.

Armitage, Angus. *Sun, Stand Thou Still*. New York: Henry Schuman, Inc., 1947.

Bevan, Rev. J. O. *University Life in Olden Times*. London: Chapman and Hall, 1914.

Bolton, Sarah K. *Famous Men of Science*. New York: Thomas Y. Crowell Company, 1889.

Clason, Clyde B. *Exploring the Distant Stars*. New York: G. P. Putnam's Sons, 1958.

Cottler, Joseph and Jaffe, Haym. *Heroes of Civilization*. Boston: Little, Brown and Company, 1931.

Eliot, George. *Romola*. New York: Oxford University Press.

Fath, Edward A. *The Elements of Astronomy*. New York: McGraw-Hill Book Co., Inc., 1955.

Gaboschkin, C. H. *Introduction to Astronomy*. New York: Prentice-Hall, Inc., 1954.

Jeans, Sir James. *Stars in Their Courses*. New York: Cambridge University Press, 1937.

———, *The Universe Around Us*. New York: Cambridge University Press, 1944.

Kahn, Fritz, *Design of the Universe*. New York: Crown Publishers, Inc., 1954.

Kesten, Hermann. *Copernicus and His World*. New York: Roy Publishers.

Kuhn, Thomas S. *The Copernican Revolution*. Cambridge: Harvard University Press, 1957.

Macpherson, Hector. *Makers of Astronomy*. Oxford: Clarendon Press, 1933.

Mitzwa, Stephen Paul. *Nicolas Copernicus*. New York: The Kosciusco Foundation, 1943.

Reichenbach, Hans. *From Copernicus to Einstein*. New York: Philosophical Library, 1942.

Shapley, Harlow. *Flights from Chaos*. New York: McGraw-Hill Book Co., Inc., 1930.

Thiel, Rudolf. *And There Was Light*. New York: Alfred A. Knopf, Inc., 1957.

Index

187

"Birth of Venus," by Botticelli, 44

Bisceglie, Duke of, 74

Bishop of Ermland, 96-102, 112, 114. *See also* Watzelrode, Lossainen, Ferber, Dantiscus

Bologna, 38, 40, 44-59, 60, 73, 79, 94, 95, 100

books and manuscripts, 24, 28-29, 45. *See also* by title

Borgia, Cesare, 73-75

Borgia, Lucrezia, 73-75

Botticelli, 44

Brahe, Tycho, 180

Braunsberg, town in Ermland, 105, 106

Brenner Pass, 40

"Broken Melody" of Poland, 17-19

brotherhood of man, Copernicus' belief in, 132-133

Brudzewski, Professor, 20-21, 22-24, 25, 34

Bruno, Giordano, 177-178

business. *See* economics

Caesar, Julius, 124

calendar, inaccuracy of, 121, 123-125; reform of, 125

Calganini, Celio, 134-135

Canon Law, Doctorate of, 72, 76-77. *See also* church law

Cardano, Jerome, 99-100

Carthage, 107

Castle of Knowledge, The, by Recorde, 177

Cathedral Academy, 16-22

Catholic Church. *See* Church

Celtes, Conrad, 22-25, 29-30, 33-34, 43, 58

Christ, 57, 124, 150

Christian Martyrs, 43

Christmas, date of. *See* calendar

Church, Catholic, 19, 61-66, 113, 119; in Poland, 9-10; tradition of, 33. *See also* Popes and Bishops

by name, Inquisition, Reformation, etc.

church law, 45. *See also* Canon Law

Clement VII, Pope, 135

coinage, Copernicus' theory of, 128-131

Colombo, Cristoforo, 31. *See also* Columbus

Columbus, 61-62. *See also* Colombo

comets, 155

commerce, 11. *See also* economics

Concerning the Revolutions of the Heavenly Spheres, by Copernicus, 10, 170, 171-175, 176, 178. *See also Revolutions sub* Copernicus

Constantinople, 45

constellations, names invented for, 83

Copernicus, 7, 8-10; childhood, 10-15, 35; birth, 11; ambition, 14; character traits, 15; early education, 16-31; patriotism, 19; adopts Latin form of name, 11, 39; early interest in astronomy, 20, 21-22, 23-25, 31, 33-37; preparation for canonship, 22, 37-38, 45; interests, 22, 27, 38; has economic security, 38-39, 77, 79; journeys to Italy, 40-44; in Bologna, 44-59, 60; career takes shape, 45-46, 64; receives leave of absence from canonship, 60, 66; legate during Jubilee Year in Rome, 61-66; studies medicine in Padua, 66-71; studies theology in Ferrara, 72-77; canon at Frauenburg, 78-92, 93-102; as practicing physician, 79-92, 97, 146-148, 156-157; writes pamphlets about his astronomical ideas, 81-87, 121; his Latin translation of Greek poems is printed, 87; establishes his observation post, 94; *Revolutions* (his lifework), 96, 104, 111, 137-140, 145, 152, 155, 158, 159-170,

190

About the Author

HENRY THOMAS was born in Latvia
and came to the United States with his
family when he was eight years old. He
attended the Boston Latin School, went
on to Harvard where he received the
degrees of A.B., A.M., and Ph.D. He has
had a varied career as teacher, editor,
publisher and writer, and has over forty
books, juvenile and adult, to his credit.
Dr. Thomas and his wife live on Long
Island.